Let Me REMEMBER YOU

God in *A Course in Miracles*

BY ROBERT PERRY AND ALLEN WATSON

#23 in a series based on *A Course in Miracles*

This is the twenty-third book in a series, each of which deals with the modern spiritual teaching *A Course in Miracles*. If you would like to receive future publications directly from the publisher, or if you would like to receive the newsletter that accompanies this series, please write us at the address below.

The Circle of Atonement
Teaching and Healing Center
P.O. Box 4238
West Sedona, AZ 86340
(520) 282-0790, Fax (520) 282-0523
E-mail: circleofa@sedona.net
Website: http://nen.sedona.net/circleofa/

The ideas presented herein are the personal interpretation and understanding of the authors, and are not necessarily endorsed by the copyright holder of *A Course in Miracles:* Foundation for Inner Peace, Inc., P.O. Box 598, Mill Valley, CA 94942.

ISBN 1-886602-13-1

Published by The Circle of Atonement: Teaching and Healing Center
Printed in the United States of America

Cover design: James L. Thompson
Typesetting, Design & Layout: Greg Mackie, Pakáage, Karen Reider

Table of
CONTENTS

The CENTRALITY of GOD

Robert

MY EXPERIENCE IS THAT GOD IS NOT DISCUSSED VERY MUCH AMONG STUDENTS OF *A COURSE IN MIRACLES*. One reason for this may be that many students come to the Course having left religious backgrounds in which God is conceived of as fearful and demanding. These students often come just wanting to take a vacation from God.

Another reason for the lack of focus on God is that, in the Course, God is so transcendental. He is so beyond the world of form that He can seem irrelevant. He therefore may be part of our story of metaphysical truth, but not part of our daily lives. For the time being, it can seem more appropriate to deal with His intermediaries: Jesus and the Holy Spirit.

Yet another reason is that, unlike many spiritual systems, the Course's focus is not on a direct approach to God, either through obedient faith, loving devotion or mystical union. Instead, its main focus is on perceiving other people differently.

For all of these reasons, and perhaps others, Course students and teachers do not seem to be absorbed with the topic of God. I doubt that one would commonly stumble on Course students deep in discussion on the nature of God, or sitting around musing about how wondrous God is, or engaged in heartfelt prayer to God. Very little is written about God's place in the Course, very little is said, and, most likely, very little is *felt*.

I have had a long-standing desire to try to do something about this state of affairs, for God stands at the absolute center of *A Course in Miracles*. We can see this simply by looking at the frequency with which the Course uses certain words. If we focus just on what could be called Course terms, like forgiveness, love, Holy Spirit, etc., the most frequently used term in the Course is God. The Course uses the word "God" 3,638 times. That is about three times for every page in the entire Course. This dwarfs the use of many other significant terms in the Course, such as miracle(s) (556), Christ (366), Holy Spirit (758), forgiveness (495), and ego (930). The only words that are used more frequently than God—with one possible exception—could hardly be classed as Course terms. These are words like "and," "for," "is," "the."

That one possible exception—the word which *is* used more frequently than God and which *might* qualify as a Course term—is "you." "You" seemed enough of a Course term to me that I included it in my *A Course Glossary*. Based on the frequency of both "you" and "God," we might consider this alternative title for the Course: *God and You*. For the Course truly is about God and you. If that claim seems far-fetched, here is another statistic: Over a quarter of all the paragraphs in the Course contain both the word "God" and the word "you."

Though these word frequencies tell us something significant, even more is told by an examination of the Course's thought system. What follows are eight points about the centrality of God in *A Course in Miracles*:

GOD IS THE SOURCE, THE CREATOR

According to the Course, everything real comes from God. He created reality itself. This is true in traditional teachings about God, yet it still bears appreciation. Everything that is real came from God's Mind and nowhere else. Theistic religions teach that this was true in the beginning, yet they also imply that once God sets the universe in motion, we have the ability to *change* His creation. For instance, He may have originally given us a pure nature, but we can corrupt that. We can give ourselves a fallen nature. This actually makes us competing creators, creating in competition with God. He is therefore not the only source, just the biggest one among many. In the Course, however, this is not so. The Course teaches that anything we make apart from God is unreal. Our making has no power to change God's original creation. His creation remains the only reality. He remains the only Source.

2 THE HEAVEN HE CREATES IS THE EXPERIENCE OF RELATIONSHIP WITH HIM

In the Course, Heaven is the sum total of reality. All else is unreal. Like other spiritualities, the Course conceives of Heaven as an abode of eternal felicity. However, unlike many popular conceptions, Heaven is not a place where, as God's servants, we go busily about our various tasks. The Course's conception is more like that of various mystical teachings, in which we simply bask in the joy of mystical union with God. The Text's closing prayer to God contains this beautiful description of the ecstatic state of Heaven: "And all creation recognizes You, and knows You as the only Source it has" (T-31.VIII.12:6).

Recognizing God, knowing God—that is the experience of Heaven. Heaven is pure knowing of God. Yet the Course also describes this same state as a song of love *to* God. "What is Heaven but a song of gratitude and love and praise by everything created to the Source of its creation?" (T-26.IV.3:5). Heaven is knowing God in mystical union and it is praising God in a song of love. And somehow these two things are actually one and the same.

Heaven is also the experience of extending God's Being, "extend[ing] the Allness and the Unity of God" (W-pI.95.12:2). Unlike the above-mentioned song, this extension seems to be away from God, an extension *outward*. Yet this extension is actually the *same thing* as our song of love to God. We can see this in the following passage: "His Son gives thanks for his creation, in the song of his creating in his Father's Name" (S-1.In.1:6). According to this passage, our song of thanks to God (the aforementioned song of love) is *also* a song of creating (or extending) in His Name. They are both the same thing.

Heaven, then, is knowing God, loving God, and extending God. Heaven is all about God.

THE SEPARATION WAS AN ATTACK ON GOD

Not only is Heaven centered on God, so was the separation, the event which gave birth to time, space and separate identity. In fact, the term "the separation" really means "the separation from God." It was an attempt to tear ourselves out of His Mind. And since God created us as part of His Mind, the separation was also a rejection of His creation of us. It was a rejection of His Authority, which had authored us as a seamless part of His Unity. In the same way that running away from home is an act directed against one's parents, so running away from Heaven was an act directed against our Father. This is why the Course calls the separation "the 'attack on God'" (T-10.V.4:2).

ALL ILLUSION IS FEAR OF AND
DEFENSE AGAINST GOD

In this world, God can seem like a very distant, irrelevant, even non-existent thing. Yet even in this world, our basic motivation—when guided by the ego—is fear of God and desire to stay away from Him. At the root of our ego's thought system, buried beneath layers of denial, is our intense fear that uniting with God means losing our identity and our existence. Thus, everything that comes out of the ego is a defense against that event. This means that all of the normal activities that make up this world have, as their underlying purpose, defending ourselves against being swallowed up in God. Our special love relationships, for instance, are really nothing more than attempts to find a substitute for disappearing into God.

ALL OUR PAIN COMES FROM THE ABSENCE OF GOD

The Course teaches that all of our pain, in one way or another, comes from the experienced absence of God. Our feelings of lack and loneliness, our sense of not being whole, and our feelings of guilt, all these seem to have more immediate causes in our everyday lives. Yet all of them ultimately stem from the belief that we are split off from our Father, our Creator, our Great Companion. This apparent split is the one source of all human misery.

ALL OUR DESIRES ARE ULTIMATELY THE DESIRE FOR GOD

This is a little-known but important teaching of the Course. The Course teaches that we are literally incapable of desiring anything except God's Love. Desires come out of our nature. Our nature produces certain desires in us. You might say that it *programs* us to have certain desires. We normally believe, for instance, that our nature programs us to be attracted to humans of the opposite sex—unless, of course, one is gay, in which case one feels programmed to be attracted to members of the *same* sex. Either way, if that is our nature, that is the way it goes. We cannot change that nature nor the desires it stirs in us.

If, however, our true nature is that we are Sons of God, then *that* nature is what gives rise to our true desires. Sons of God want only God. Because of their nature, He is the only thing they want. And He, says the Course, is the only thing *we* want. We are actually incapable of wanting anything else. This is true right now and has always been true. Even when we think we want money or food or status or sex, the desire *inside* those desires is for God. We think we want those things only because the ego has tricked us into believing that they will deliver some taste of the Love of God. The fact that we don't *really* want those things is revealed by what happens when we actually get them: We aren't satisfied. They don't do it for us. Only the experience of God's Love puts all of our desires to rest. That is the proof that His Love is what we really want. Only within His embrace do we truly rest from wanting.

The following prayer from the Course expresses these ideas beautifully:

> *What can I seek for, Father, but Your Love? Perhaps I think I seek for something else; a something I have called by many names. Yet is Your Love the only thing I seek, or ever sought. For there is nothing else that I could ever really want to find.* (W-pII.231.1:1–4)

7 GOD IS THE MEANS OF OUR AWAKENING

While we dream of being away from God, living in a physical world, God is the One Who guides us home. Course students generally understand the role of guiding us home as being the Holy Spirit's. And this, of course, is correct. However, it would also be correct to say that God is doing so *through* the Holy Spirit. What is *not* correct is seeing God as totally passive in relation to our homecoming. The Course is quite clear that He responds to the separation. He answers it. He creates the Holy Spirit to heal it. He establishes the plan of salvation, which the Holy Spirit carries out. He speaks His saving Word to us through His Voice (the Holy Spirit). He even walks beside us (as we will discuss in Chapter 10). He promises to hear our calls and answer every one. We will discuss God's relationship to the Holy Spirit more fully in Chapter 8. For now, we might simply say that the Holy Spirit is God's gesture of reaching out to us in our separated condition.

GOD IS THE GOAL
OF OUR AWAKENING

If Heaven is all about God, and if the goal of the spiritual journey is to reawaken to Heaven, then that goal is also to awaken to God. He is the endpoint toward which we journey. He is the end of our labors. One of the Course's prayers says this about the end of the spiritual journey: "The memory of You awaits me there. And all my sorrows end in Your embrace" (W-pII.317.2:4–5).

Our whole goal is to reach that place where we remember God, where total knowledge of Him rises from the repressed depths of our mind and we again know Him face-to-face. In that experience all our sorrows will end, because our sorrows were nothing more than the absence of His Presence. In that experience all our yearnings will rest, for those yearnings were nothing but the longing for His Love.

These eight points explain why the Course mentions God 3638 times. The whole Course revolves around Him like planets around the sun, just as it claims reality revolves around Him. The Course is all about God; or, as we said, it is all about God and you. It is about your orbit around Him: your true orbit, your attempt to stray from that orbit, and your ultimate return to it.

God is everyone's central concern, whether they realize it or not

Most people do not go through their day thinking that their whole existence is about God. As we saw earlier, neither do most Course students. However, according to the Course's teaching, God is the central concern for everyone, whether they know it or not. Because He is the Creator of our minds and the Substance of our minds, all our thinking and feeling will inevitably be saturated with Him, even if we are unaware of this. Consequently, our daily thoughts are filled with desiring, resenting, and fearing Him, even while it seems we are thinking about other things. Those apparent thoughts about other things are really disguised thoughts about Him.

The following passage captures the exact nature of our hidden universal preoccupation with God:

> No right mind can believe that its will is stronger than God's. If, then, a mind believes that its will is different from His, it can only decide either that there is no God or that God's Will is fearful. The former accounts for the atheist and the latter for the martyr, who believes that God demands sacrifices. Either of these insane decisions will induce panic, because the atheist believes he is alone, and the martyr believes that God is crucifying him. Yet no one really wants either abandonment or retaliation, even though many may seek both. (T-9.I.8:1–5)

I find this to be a fascinating passage, just as whenever the Course comments on specific phenomena in this world. What I see in this passage is an implied contrast between the atheist and the martyr's conscious attitudes, on the one hand, and their underlying beliefs, on the other. Let's take the two cases one at a time.

On a conscious level, the martyr is saying, "I love God. Out of my love for Him I will sacrifice anything for Him. I will even die for Him." Yet underneath this passionate profession are darker beliefs: "The martyr believes that God is crucifying him," and "believes that God demands sacrifices." In short, the martyr lives in fear of a cruel God Who demands death as the price of loving Him.

Now let's look at the atheist. On a conscious level, he is saying, "I don't believe that God exists." The atheist, in other words, "believes he is alone" in the universe. But notice how this idea of being alone is rephrased in the final sentence. It is called "abandonment." In other words, underneath the conscious level, the atheist believes he is alone, not because there is no God, but because God *abandoned* him. The atheist *does* believe in God. He believes in a God Who left him.

We need to pause right here and appreciate this last idea. If even the atheist believes in God, then there *are* no genuine atheists. We all believe in God; that is, the cruel God that we made up. The Course seems to allude to this idea again a few sections later in the following passage:

> Projecting condemnation onto God, they [theologians] make Him appear retaliative, and fear His retribution....It is understandable that there have been revolts against this concept, but to revolt against it is still to believe in it. (T-9.V.3:5,7)

The revolts the Course is talking about here are almost certainly the modern revolts against the traditional Western God, which would definitely include atheism. Thus, even those who are revolting against the tyrannical God of western religion still believe in Him, and are showing it *by* their revolt.

There is one final level, and it is one that both the martyr and the atheist share. Deep down, each of their minds "believes that its will is different from His," from God's. Each one of them believes that he has violated God's Will. This explains why Jesus calls their two stances "abandonment" and "retaliation." Both stances are rooted in the expectation of Divine payback. Underneath it all, the atheist believes that he has sinned against God and that, as payment, God has *abandoned* him. The martyr believes that he has sinned against God and that, as payment, God is *retaliating* against him. Both stances come from the same source: deep-seated feelings of guilt. As the Course says earlier, "Guilt feelings… induce fears of retaliation or abandonment" (T-5.VI.2:1–2).

The atheist and the martyr seem to be poles apart. They seem to embody the two furthest extremes on the issue of God. One is willing to die for God. The other has decided there is no God. What could they possibly have in common? Everything, says the Course. In fact, they are really not different at all. Both have the same buried belief: that they have sinned against God and that, as a result, He has dished out payback. Only the form of the payback differs. Yet regardless of the form, this belief in vengeance from God will have the same emotional result. It "will induce panic" in both atheist and martyr, as our above passage says.

If two such opposite poles believe the same thing, obviously everyone in between does, too. Everyone believes it. Whatever our formal beliefs, we all carry out our lives on top of a single massive assumption: that we have sinned against God and that He will get us back.

This same belief explains why we are unaware of this assumption. To see how this belief leads directly to being unaware of it, let us turn to the following passage:

> Who usurps the place of God and takes it for himself now has a deadly "enemy." And he must stand alone in his protection, and make himself a shield to keep him safe from fury that can never be abated, and vengeance that can never be satisfied.
>
> How can this unfair battle be resolved? Its ending is inevitable, for its outcome must be death. How, then, can one believe in one's defenses? Magic again must help. Forget the battle. Accept it as a fact, and then forget it. Do not remember the impossible odds against you. Do not remember the immensity of the "enemy," and do not think about your frailty in comparison. Accept your separation, but do not remember how it came about. Believe that you have won it, but do not retain the slightest memory of Who your great "opponent" really is. Projecting your "forgetting" onto Him, it seems to you He has forgotten, too. (M-17.5:8–6:11)

This passage bears close scrutiny. If you truly believe that you have displaced God as your Creator and become your own creator (which we all unconsciously believe), then you also believe that you have made God into your enemy. And what a terrifying enemy! In such a battle, you can only lose. The odds are utterly impossible. What do you do?

What do so many of us do now when faced with a completely hopeless situation, one that we are convinced can never be solved nor won? We mentally sweep it under the rug. We push it down in our minds and hope that this pushes it out of existence itself. We forget it and hope it goes away. We close our eyes and hope that it can't see us. And that, says the above passage, is exactly what we did with our problem with God. We assumed that the problem was fully real and exactly as we had defined it. We assumed that we had made an omnipotent enemy Who would never stop until He had exacted every last drop of His bloody revenge. And then, as a defense against this horrifying fear, we tried desperately to forget the whole thing, and we succeeded.

And now we look around us and see no God. We look within and feel no God. We conduct our lives without much thought of God. Even the most religious among us are spending most of our time thinking about something else. We wonder why God is so strangely absent, so nonchalantly remote. The question of whether there is a God seems to be a real question, one with no proven answer. The whole issue of God seems to be one that we can pick or put down by our own choice.

We don't realize that this is all a ruse, a trick of the mind. We don't realize that we *had* to make a world in which God seemed to be an optional issue, an elective. We had to do so because, underneath the conscious level, every one of us exists in mortal terror that God is out to pay us back for a primordial sin of metaphysical proportions. We don't realize that we are all conducting our lives on top of an ancient argument with God. And we especially don't realize that, underneath that argument, He is our eternal Love in Whom we live and move and have our being.

2

Basic THEOLOGY

Allen

THEOLOGY, OF COURSE, IS "THE STUDY OF THE NATURE OF GOD AND RELIGIOUS TRUTH." This whole book, since it is about God in *A Course in Miracles*, is theological in nature. In this chapter, however, I am going to zero in on what the Course says specifically about God: God's nature, God's characteristics, God's attributes.

This sort of discussion may seem abstract and remote at times; I apologize if you find it dry. I am going to do my best to show how each of these aspects is meaningful and relevant to our mundane lives in this world. It is important, however, as we move into the later discussion of our relationship with God, to have a clear idea of *What*, or *Whom*, we are in relationship with. These points about God are the assumptions and presuppositions upon which the Course bases everything else it has to say about God, and about our involvement with God. These are the foundation stones of the building. We need to know what the foundation is before we build on it. Once we have a building going, we may not need to spend much time discussing the foundation, but having a firm foundation is crucial to building an understanding of God that will endure.

God IS.

The first, rather obvious, point about God is simply that God exists. *God is.* The Course does not attempt to prove or justify the existence of God; it simply assumes it. For example:

> Oneness is simply the idea God is. And in His Being, He encompasses all things. No mind holds anything but Him. We say "God is," and then we cease to speak, for in that knowledge words are meaningless. (W-pI.169.5:1-4)

The idea that "words are meaningless" may distract us at the outset. If we take that in an absolute sense, then everything in this book, which is basically a lot of words about God, is meaningless. I may as well stop writing; you may as well stop reading! Yet it cannot mean that. If it did, most of the Course itself would be meaningless; the only words that count would be "God is."

The paragraph is talking about the time when we have been restored to total conscious union with God. *In that level of experience,* when we have moved from perception into full knowledge, all that is necessary is "God is." Nothing else means anything, because in conscious union with God we realize that there *is* nothing else but God. All is God, and therefore anything else, any other words, mean nothing. That experience of oneness is our destination, our goal. In that union,

> There are no lips to speak them [words], and no part of mind sufficiently distinct to feel that it is now aware of something not itself. It has united with its Source. And like its Source Itself, it merely is. (W-pI.169.5:5-7)

Now, however, when our minds are quite sufficiently distinct (or seem to be) and are aware of *lots* of things that are not part of mind, words *are* meaningful. Now, words can help us move along the journey, and clear up our perceptions to the point at which God can take the last step, and translate our perception into this final knowledge. So our discussion of theology *does* have relevance!

Yet are the words but aids, and to be used...but to recall the mind, as needed, to its purpose....We use the words, and try and try again to go beyond them to their meaning, which is far beyond their sound. (W-pI.rV.In.12:1,4)

Consider what the words of this paragraph from Lesson 169 are telling us. The ultimate knowledge is simply that "God is," and there is nothing else; "In His Being, He encompasses all things." The highest revelation, the deepest awareness of the truth of all existence, is simply that God is All That Is. There is nothing else.

The Course makes this assertion, or simply assumes it, in several places:

God is All in all in a very literal sense. All being is in Him Who is all Being. (T-7.IV.7:4-5)

He is All in all. (T-8.IV.1:4)

Heaven is not a place nor a condition. It is merely an awareness of perfect oneness, and the knowledge that there is nothing else; nothing outside this oneness, and nothing else within. (T-18.VI.1:5-6)

You may also want to read T-8.V.3:1; T-14.VIII.5:2; and W-pI.95.12:2.

The Course tells us, later in Lesson 169, that in our present state we cannot comprehend oneness; we cannot even speak nor write nor think of it at all. We can only approximate it. Oneness will simply return to our mind when we have finished what we need to do here. "Now we have work to do," it says (W-pI.169.10:3), and we do not need to waste our time speculating about what that experience of oneness is like. When it comes to us, we will know, and that will be enough.

Our purpose here, in this book about God in *A Course in Miracles*, is not to pontificate on the subtleties and profundities of oneness. We just want to become utterly clear that underlying everything the Course is saying, there is a fundamental assumption that *God is*. Nothing exists outside of God; all His creations are part of Himself. Since that is true, it means that from the Course's point of view, all of reality is in God. I am in God; you are in God; your favorite enemy is in God. There is, quite literally, nowhere else to be, because all being is in God. *God is*, and only God is.

All else that the Course has to teach us is based upon this single, profound fact. It colors everything the Course says about forgiveness and salvation and the healing of relationships. Fully understood, those two simple words, *God is*, could bring us to complete enlightenment.

God, and all God creates, are eternal

Another assumption the Course makes is that God, and all of God's creations, are eternal. The Course does not expect this to be questioned; it is stated as fact. Since God is eternal, and His creations are part of Himself, then those creations must also be eternal.

> God is as incapable of creating the perishable as the ego is of
> making the eternal.   (T-4.I.11:7)

The Course uses this very assumption of the eternal nature of God's creations as proof of the world's unreality. God does not create anything changeable or perishable, or anything that ends. That eliminates the entire physical universe, because even galaxies end. Therefore, God did not create them; nor did he create the Earth, or our short-lived bodies:

> The world as you perceive it cannot have been created by the
> Father, for the world is not as you see it. God created only the
> eternal, and everything you see is perishable. Therefore, there
> must be another world that you do not see.
>   (T-11.VII.1:1-3; see also C-4.1:1-5)

Before we move on from this point I want to talk a little about what "eternal" means. We commonly think of eternity as a very long time, or time without ending. But eternity has nothing to do with time at all. Time is a thing of beginnings and endings; time is the context that makes change possible. To say God is eternal means that God exists outside of time, without any beginning, without change, and without ending. God simply is. Therefore, to say that God's creations are eternal means the same thing: They exist outside of time, they have nothing to do with time, they do not change, and they have no beginning or ending.

God's creations have always been, because He has always been.
(T-7.I.3:7)

Therefore, whatever exists only within time does not exist at all except as an illusion; it is not real because it is not eternal, and God creates nothing but the eternal. Yet what is real exists forever, apart from time. If you and I exist, therefore, we must be eternal beings! It is this kind of thinking that gave the biblical Psalmist and Moses such confidence:

God [is] our refuge and strength, a very present help in trouble.
Therefore will not we fear, though the earth be removed, and though the mountains be carried into the midst of the sea.
(Ps. 46:1-2)

The eternal God [is thy] refuge, and underneath [are] the everlasting arms.
(Deut. 33:27)

This conception that reality and eternal existence are wholly congruent-all that is real is eternal, and only what is eternal is real-is the basis for the first of the Course's concise self-summaries:

This course can therefore be summed up very simply in this way:
Nothing real can be threatened.
Nothing unreal exists.
(T-In.2:1-3)

If God is eternal, so are you. If everything real is eternal, then nothing real can be threatened. There can be no danger. There is nothing to fear. Things that come and go, shift and change, or suffer and die, are for that very reason not real, and their "loss" not a real loss. Nothing real has been lost; nothing real *can* be lost.

God is formless

God has no form but He does use forms. The Course speaks of "the forms which never can deceive, because they come from Formlessness Itself" (W-pI.186.14:1), which is an obvious reference to God ("Formlessness") and the way in which the gifts of formless Love take on the form "most useful in a world of form" (W-pI.186.13:5). God's Love is formless, but in a world of form, it "takes on" form to meet our needs.

God does not create forms. How could He, if He is formless, and everything He creates is part of Himself? And yet there are forms in this world that appear to come from God. How can that be? The Course explains:

> Creation cannot even be conceived of in the world....For being Heaven-born, it has no form at all. Yet God created One Who has the power to translate in form the wholly formless. What He makes are dreams, but of a kind so close to waking that the light of day already shines in them, and eyes already opening behold the joyful sights their offerings contain.
>
> (W-pI.192.3:1,4-6)

The "One" God created is the Holy Spirit. He takes the formless and, from it, makes forms, or dreams (because everything in the world of form is a dream). By means of these forms, which perfectly reflect the formless Love of God, we can begin to see the Love of God they represent. The Holy Spirit bridges the gap; He translates between formlessness and form; and very clearly, He *does* operate in the world of form, although God Himself does not do so directly.

God is formless. Yet the Course tells us, "You cannot even think of God without a body, or in some form you think you recognize" (T-18.VIII.1:7). All of our concepts of God, as long as we are in this world of form, will be made up of some "form" in which we think of God. We may think of God as a body, or as an invisible field of pure energy. We may think of God as a Mind, or as an Ideal Person. The idea of God's formlessness, however, can remind us that none of these forms are, in fact, God. They may be the best we can do to represent God in our thoughts, but they are not, actually, God.

We need to be careful that, in our thinking about God, we do not mistake the forms for God: that we do not, for instance, let the image of a body cause us to think of God as male, or as female. Nor should the image of God as an energy field cause us to believe God is actually a part of, or the basis of, the physical universe. He is not any of the forms we use to represent Him. God is not a "He," nor a "She."

Thirty or more years ago an Anglican clergyman, J. B. Phillips, wrote a book called *Your God is Too Small.* In it, he said we all had our definitions of God, which he called "God in a box." That phrase has always stuck with me as a picture of what happens when we think we have captured God in some form. "God in a box." God is not any form. God is formless. You cannot pin down the form of God, because any form limits God and diminishes God.

God creates by extending Himself

If God is formless, and God does not create form, what does He create, and how? The Course tells us that God creates by extending Himself. He, the Loving One, extends more Love. He, the Living One, extends more life. He extends His Being. And what He creates is, therefore, exactly like Himself. What He creates is still and forever a part of Himself.

> To extend is a fundamental aspect of God which He gave to His Son. In the creation, God extended Himself to His creations and imbued them with the same loving Will to create. (T-2.I.1:1-2)

Extending, the Course tells us, is "a fundamental aspect of God." In this passage we can see that "to extend" and "the loving

Will to create" are close synonyms. To create is to extend; to extend is to create. And extension, or creation, is closely allied to *love*. Extension is a loving activity, and loving is an extending activity.

> God created His Sons by extending His Thought, and retaining the extensions of His Thought in His Mind. (T-6.II.8:1)

We were created by God extending His Thought; He *thought* us into being. We are, then, Thoughts in God's Mind, and those Thoughts were retained in God's Mind; we exist there, in the Mind of God, and that is the entirety of our existence. Therefore, God's Thought of you *is* you, it is what you are.

> The Thought God holds of you remains exactly as it always was....the Thought God holds of you has never left the Mind of its Creator. (T-30.III.10:2,5)

This is why "I remain as God created me" (W-pI.139.11:3). God's creations are not separate from Him; they are *part* of Him, and they *cannot* become anything else. They live, exist, and have their being in His Mind; His creations are His Thoughts, and cannot leave His Mind: "Ideas leave not their source." (In Chapter 4, we will expand on the importance to us of God as Creator.)

Extension is a fundamental aspect of God. That is, it lies at the heart of what God is. It is part of His nature. To extend is to give of oneself, in the most literal sense possible: To somehow actually have a part of yourself go out to become something more of you than was there before.

God's extension is compared to the "inner radiance" of His Sons (T-2.I.2:4). The use of the word "radiance" suggests *light*. Creation is like the shining of the Sun; light is continually going forth from the Sun, and yet that light is nothing more than a part of the Sun, an extension of it. We, God's creations, are in relation to Him as the light is to the Sun. We are His radiance, shining outward, ever extending, never depleted. Shining is what the Sun does; extension is what God "does."

Yet the analogy falls short, because, while light can be seen as an extension of the Sun, light itself does not have the power to extend itself in more light. But we, God's creations, have the function of extending as He extends; He has extended even that to us.

> God has given you a place in His Mind that is yours forever. Yet you can keep it only by giving it, as it was given you....God's Mind cannot be lessened. It can only be increased, for everything He creates has the function of creating....To give without limit is God's Will for you, because only this can bring you the joy that is His and that He wills to share with you. Your love is as boundless as His because it *is* His.
>
> ...could any part of His Love be contained?....God wills to create, and your will is His. It follows, then, that you will to create, since your will follows from His. And being an extension of His Will, yours must be the same. (T-11.I.6-7, selected)

Thus, this "fundamental aspect" of God, extending Himself in loving creation, is also a fundamental aspect of what we are; His nature determines ours, and defines our function as identical to God's.

God is changeless

God's nature is to create, to extend Himself. And yet, in some paradoxical way, God is also changeless. Constantly creating, He remains the same.

> What is timeless is always there, because its being is eternally changeless. It does not change by increase, because it was forever created to increase. If you perceive it as not increasing you do not know what it is. (T-7.I.7:9-11)

God increases by creation, but He does not change, because increase is His nature; it is what God is, part of His very Being. Extension is closely aligned with love, as we have seen, and love is described in the Course as constantly extending, increasing, and yet unchanging:

> [Love] is changeless but continually exchanged, being offered
> by the eternal to the eternal. In this exchange it is extended, for
> it increases as it is given. (T-13.V.1:2-3)

If we think of love, then this concept of something extending, being exchanged, and increasing, and yet being changeless, can begin to be grasped. As we give love, love is not lost, nor is love changed, and yet it increases. The exchange of love between the Sons of God is a reflection of creation in this world. *The Song of Prayer* expresses this connection between love and creation like this:

> Endless the harmony, and endless, too, the joyous concord of
> the Love They give forever to Each Other. And in this, creation
> is extended. God gives thanks to His extension in His Son. His
> Son gives thanks for his creation, in the song of his creating in
> his Father's Name. (S-1.In.1:3-6)

God, then, along with His creations, is engaged in an endless, changeless exchange of love. It is a song of gratitude, of concord or union, and of thanks, endlessly, changelessly being sung, an eternal current of love.

God is omnipotent, omniscient, and omnipresent

There are three other aspects of God that are assumed by the Course, along with most traditional theology. I call them the three "omni's": omnipotent, omniscient, and omnipresent. They mean, basically, all-powerful, all-knowing, and everywhere present.

They follow logically from an earlier characteristic: that God is literally All in All. If nothing but God exists, He therefore must be all-powerful, since there is nothing to oppose Him. He must be all-knowing, since He knows Himself as All. And He must be omnipresent, since there is nothing and nowhere outside of Him. Unlike older views, however, God is not one thing among many, somehow still all-powerful despite being opposed. God is the *only* power, the *only* place, and the *only* subject and object of knowledge.

An "idol" is anything that we set up and imagine to be somehow contradictory to God's uniqueness, to any of these "omni's." The Course speaks of idols, and in so doing, makes it clear that God alone has power, existence, and presence—God, along with His creations, His Sons, who are part of Him:

> This is the anti-Christ; the strange idea there is a power past omnipotence, a place beyond the infinite, a time transcending the eternal. (T-29.VIII.6:2)

The paragraph goes on to say that the world is a place set up in illusory opposition to God, to challenge His omnipotence, to be a place where God is not—"a place beyond the infinite"—and to be a place where God's creations, changeless as He is, suffer change and loss. This is a concept we will explore later when we discuss the ego's attack on God.

God is intensely personal

The aspects of God we've considered so far may seem to give a picture of a God Who is so different from us He is impossible to understand, and so vastly distant He can never be reached. How can I feel close to a God Who knows nothing of form? How can I, knowing nothing but form, relate to a God Who is formless? Formlessness seems to imply "impersonal." Many Course students, in fact, have said that they think of God as a sort of impersonal Force, the great Original Cause. There seems to be little possibility of a personal relationship with such a God.

The Course gives another side of God, however. It portrays a God Who, although formless, is also *intensely personal,* and a God with Whom we can relate in intimate, loving ways.

Robert suggests that we think of the various ideas of God as a line of possible conceptions. On the left end of the line is the "impersonal force." As you progress towards the middle of the line, you begin to see God as a "big person," somewhat like the Greek idea of Zeus or, a bit further along the line, the biblical concept of Jehovah. In getting away from this "big person" idea, the Course would not have us return to the left end of the line, back to the idea of an impersonal force. That makes God *less than* a person. Rather, we should go all the way in the opposite direction. We take all the added aspects of personhood and amplify them to an infinite degree. This God is not a big person, nor less than a person. Rather, He is infinitely more.

The Course freely employs human symbols such as father to refer to God; some related material in *The Gifts of God*, scribed just like the Course material, even uses mother, lover, or brother:

> Rest could be yours because of what God is. He loves you as a mother loves her child; her only one, the only love she has, her all-in-all, extension of herself, as much a part of her as breath itself. He loves you as a brother loves his own; born of one father, still as one in him, and bonded with a seal that cannot break. He loves you as a lover loves his own; his chosen one, his joy, his very life, the one he seeks when she has gone away, and brings him peace again on her return. He loves you as a father loves his son, without whom would his self be incomplete, whose immortality completes his own.
>
> *(The Gifts of God*, page 126)

Such personal symbols are used because they convey something crucial about God. They say that a person is a better symbol for God than is an impersonal force or energy field. Like a person, God has a mind, awareness, intelligence, will, and emotion, but God has them to an infinite degree. This God *loves* His creations.

In Lesson 346 we are given a prayer in which we are led to say, "I would forget all things except Your Love" (W-pII.346.1:5).

In Lesson 324 we pray:

Father, You are the One Who gave the plan for my salvation to me.
You have set the way I am to go, the role to take, and every step in my
appointed path. I cannot lose the way. I can but choose to wander off
a while, and then return. Your loving Voice will always call me back .
(W-pII.324.1:1-5)

These are not words one would speak to an impersonal Force; these are the words of a loving Son to his Loving Father. The very use of the term, "Father," implies one of the closest of personal relationships. (Robert will expand on the Father–Son relationship and what it implies in the next chapter.)

In Lesson 317, we say, "All my sorrows end in Your embrace" (W-pII.317.2:5). God *embraces* us; what a strongly *personal* feeling there is in that word! Of course it is a metaphor, a figure of speech, since if God has no body, He has no arms with which to embrace us. But figures of speech *mean something.* The dictionary says that a figure of speech is intended to achieve an effect that is beyond the range of ordinary language. They convey *more* than direct words can convey. To speak of God's embrace, then, tells us that God relates to us in a very direct and personal manner. An impersonal Force does not embrace you; only a personal being, with a personal interest in and affection for you, embraces you.

The Course speaks several times of God smiling upon us. For example:

Father, Your Son is holy. I am he on whom You smile in love and ten-
derness so dear and deep and still the universe smiles back on You,
and shares Your Holiness. How pure, how safe, how holy, then, are
we, abiding in Your Smile, with all Your Love bestowed upon us, liv-
ing one with You, in brotherhood and Fatherhood complete.
(W-pII.341.1:1-3)

That image is certainly not an impersonal image. It is *intense-ly personal.* We live, "abiding in Your Smile." God sees us, He knows us, He loves what He sees, and He smiles upon us; we can bask in that smile, happily aware of His loving approval, His tender care for us.

In Chapters 1 and 4 of the Text, the Course speaks about revelation, which is an experience in which we are in direct communication with God. While revelation is not held up as something to be sought after–it comes when it comes–three times we are told that the experience of revelation is "intensely personal" or a "highly personal experience." We are told that revelation involves "the extremely personal sense of creation sometimes sought in physical relationships" (T-1.II.1:2). That is a clear reference to sexual intercourse. Revelation is *that* personal! In fact, I suspect that the union of God with His creations experienced in revelation is what we are attempting to recreate in sexual union; it is the original experience we seek to duplicate in a physical way.

God is not an impersonal Force, nor is our relationship with God meant to be an impersonal relationship. It can be intensely personal, highly personal, extremely personal. God is with us, in us, around us in every direction.

> God is with me. He is my Source of life, the life within, the air I breathe, the food by which I am sustained, the water which renews and cleanses me. He is my home, wherein I live and move; the Spirit Which directs my actions, offers me Its Thoughts, and guarantees my safety from all pain. He covers me with kindness and with care, and holds in love the Son He shines upon, who also shines on Him. How still is he who knows the truth of what He speaks today!   (W-pII.222.1:1-5)

In reality, nothing is more personal than God. Nothing is more personal than our relationship with Him. Every other form of intimacy is a poor second to the intimacy between God and His creations; in fact, "The holy relationship reflects the true relationship the Son of God has with his Father in reality" (T-20.VI.10:1). All our relationships are destined to become holy, and every holy relationship has as its purpose only to teach us the true degree of intimacy and personalness that exists in our relationship to God:

> You are forever in a relationship so holy that it calls to everyone to escape from loneliness, and join you in your love. And where you are must everyone seek, and find you there.
>
> (T-15.VIII.3:8-9)

And let Him Whose teaching is only of God teach you the only meaning of relationships. For God created the only relationship that has meaning, and that is His relationship with you (T-15.VIII.6:5-6).

God is loving

That leads us to our final point: God is loving. I'm only going to touch on this lightly; space does not permit much more, despite its importance.

"God is but Love" (W-pI.rV.In.4:3), the Course tells us. As in most instances where the Course uses the word "but" in this sense, it could be replaced with the word "only": "God is *only* Love." How could a God Who is Love be anything but personal? How could a personal God be anything but loving?

The Bible, as most of us know, agrees with the idea; the Epistle of John tells us several times that "God is Love." The Course, however, by adding that word "but," extends the meaning. It is saying, God is Love and only Love, nothing else.

We are asked to "feel the Love of God within" us now (W-pI.189.Heading). Simply to feel the Love of God is to know the real world; to feel the Love of God transforms our perception. So much is based on the fact that God is Love. Our very nature derives from it: "God is but Love, and therefore so am I" (W-pI.rV.In.4:3). The Course's interpretation of the crucifixion is based on the thought that no loving Father would make the way to Him depend on death and sacrifice (See T-3.I, "Atonement without Sacrifice"). Love is what draws us home; the attraction of love within us for God's Love is irresistible. "Our Love awaits us as we go to Him," says Lesson 302.

SUMMARY

So, to recap: God IS—He *is* Being, He is the All in All, perfectly One. God is eternal and formless, always extending in creation, yet changeless and outside of time. He is omnipotent, omniscient, and omnipresent. And yet God is intensely personal, and above all else, God is Love.

3

FATHER and SON

Robert

THE COURSE'S PRIMARY LANGUAGE FOR OUR RELATIONSHIP WITH GOD IS THAT OF FATHER AND SON. There are over 800 references to God as Father and over 1300 references to ourselves as His Son. Why does the Course use this language? What is this language trying to communicate about our relationship with God? And how does this language relate to the traditional language of God the Father and His Son?

THE SYMBOL OF THE
IDEAL FATHER-SON RELATIONSHIP

The relationship between father and son is one of the richest cultural images we have, one filled with deeply emotional connotations. The Course takes this rich and complex image and uses it as a symbol for our relationship with God. This symbol, therefore, must have something crucial to tell us. It must be able to implant essential truths in our minds. We are currently unable to comprehend our true relationship with God. It is a transcendental thing, beyond the scope of our tiny human minds. I believe the Course uses the symbol of the earthly father-son relationship to carry our minds toward that which we currently cannot conceive. It seems to serve as a way to stir in our minds a distant memory of a relationship which once meant everything to us, but which now is almost completely unconscious.

Let us, therefore, examine the earthly father-son relationship. If we can understand what it is, then we can gain a sense of what it symbolizes. As we begin, bear in mind that the Course is employing the symbol of the *ideal* father-son relationship. It is not concerned with the abusive father, the disapproving father, the negligent father, nor the absent father. It is drawing on an image, which I believe we all have, of the *perfect* father.

What is the essence of how a father regards his son? A father views his son as an extension of his own identity. In fathering his son, the father's very identity seems to have expanded out to produce more of itself in the world. Now, a miniature version of the father exists. The son, though different from his father in some ways, inevitably carries some essential likenesses. He is to some degree, as the saying goes, "a chip off the old block." The son is an extension of his father's identity.

As such, the son will somehow complete the father. By extending outward and fathering a reflection of itself, the father's identity has become more. It has increased. And this increase completes the father's identity, a fact which shows up in a feeling of fulfillment.

This extension also continues the father. It carries on the father's identity. The son will, it is hoped, grant the father a kind of immortality in a world of mortality. Even though the father must die, he has the comfort of knowing that he will in some sense live on through his son, and through his son's sons. His identity will somehow continue through the extensions of that identity.

The son, therefore, is the *extension, completion, and continuation of his father.* And this evokes a very simple and obvious thing from the father: *He loves his son.* How could he not love the extension, completion, and continuation of his own identity? The father looks upon his son as his joy, his treasure, the apple of his eye. A father's love for his son is one of the central facts of this world. Fathers love their sons; not all fathers, and rarely as much as they would like. But even in the most painful father-son relationships, there is some tiny spark of real fatherly love. And, of course, there are those father-son relationships in which pure love is no mere spark, but the dominant theme of the relationship. Those are the relationships the Course is drawing upon for its symbol. Please bear with me in exploring these relationships in a little more detail, for they speak volumes about how God views His relationship to us.

This love of the father's manifests in countless ways. The father gives his son whatever he needs, making sure he lacks nothing. He puts a roof over his head, makes certain he is clothed and does not go hungry. The father is a refuge, a place of safety. He protects his son from a cruel world, from the elements, and from the son's own carelessness and inexperience. When the son needs help, he can always count on his father being there. When the son does not know the way, his father takes him by the hand and leads him. The father's guidance is crucial in the son becoming a full person who is able to stand on his own two feet. Even more important is the father's love and acceptance. When the son makes mistakes, the ideal father forgives him. When the son sins, the door to home is always open.

In the end, the loving father gives his son everything he has. Nothing is held back. Why would the father hold anything back when the son is the extension, completion, and continuation of his own identity? The father passes his name on to his son and so identifies the son with him; he gives the son his own identity. The father also passes on his station in life, his place in the world. This may be as general as the son simply receiving the opportunities granted by his father's status—opportunities that will allow the son to achieve a similar place in society. Or it may be as specific as the son carrying on his father's particular occupation, even taking over the family business. Finally, the father eventually passes on to his son whatever wealth and property he has accumulated over the course of his life.

Hence, with his father's name, station in life, wealth, and property, the son eventually becomes the visible continuation of his father. He becomes the living legacy of the man who gave him everything, including life itself.

All of the above has to do with how the father relates to his son. Consider also, in such an ideal father-son relationship, how would the son feel toward the father? This may take some thought to answer, since we are so used to sons feeling alienated and resentful toward their fathers. Yet such feelings would not have much room to grow in the ideal relationship I just outlined. In that relationship, the son would feel immensely grateful. He has received everything that he has from his father: his sustenance, his safety, his guidance, his place in the world, his name, his very life. What could this inspire but a gratitude that lived in the son's heart as a cornerstone of his existence? He would also feel trust. He would know that he could rely on his father's wisdom, guidance, help, and love. He would know that his father would always be there for him. Rather than trying to be as different as possible, the son would want to be like his father, and be glad that he *is* like his father, whatever differences may also exist. Rather than get as far away as he could, the son would want to be near his father, even when he has grown up and had his own sons. All of these feelings would be aspects of the one feeling that encapsulates them all: *The son would love his father.* Just as the father began by loving his son, so in return the son would love his father.

And thus the cycle would be complete. The father loves his son for extending, completing, and continuing his identity. The son loves his father for supplying, sustaining, and protecting *his* identity.

APPLYING THE EARTHLY FATHER-SON RELATIONSHIP TO THE DIVINE

As I hope the previous section made clear, the father-son relationship is one of the richest and most powerful images this world has to offer. The Course makes use of every bit of this image. In calling God our Father and us His Son, the Course is not just referring to the fact that God fathered or created us. It is saying much, much more. It is drawing upon the father-son image in its entirety. In fact, even though I am a father myself, the picture I painted above came only partially from my own experience as a father and from my observations of human culture. It mostly came from reflecting on a wealth of comments the Course itself drops about the nature of the father-son relationship. The Course, it seems, is intimately familiar with every nuance of this relationship. And, as I said, it uses this familiarity to the hilt. Every single thing we just said about the earthly father-son relationship gets pressed into service as a symbol for the divine Father-Son relationship.

To see this in action, let us now examine a series of passages from the Course in which earthly fathers and sons are used as a symbol for the heavenly Father and Son.

An exclamation of fatherly love

> How lovely are you, Child of Holiness! How like to Me! How lovingly I hold you in My Heart and in My Arms. How dear is every gift to Me that you have made, who healed My Son and took him from the cross. (S-3.IV.9:4–7)

This passage actually comes from *The Song of Prayer*, a supplement to the Course scribed by the same source through Helen Schucman. *The Song of Prayer* closes with a page-long communication in which the first person is God. Notice the fatherly language in the above passage. We can easily picture a loving father exclaiming to his child how beautiful (or handsome) he is, how like his father he is. We can see the father lovingly holding his child in his arms and in his heart. We can see him treasuring every little gift his child has made for him, even a simple scribble on a piece of paper.

The Course takes this commonplace imagery and gives it a transcendental meaning. "How lovely are you," refers not to your physical appearance, but to your non-physical radiance as a "Child of Holiness." You are an extension of the pure, boundless light of God's Holiness. That is your true loveliness.

"How like to Me" does not refer to your body or your personality being similar to your earthly father's. It refers to the fact that you are an extension of God's Spirit. Being made of His Spirit, you are more than like Him; you are *identical* to Him.

God holding you in His Arms is not a physical act, for He has no physical arms. The Course uses the image of being wrapped in God's Arms as a symbol for being enfolded in His limitless protection, peace, and Love. For aren't these the things we feel when wrapped in a father's arms?

When an earthly father holds you in his heart, it simply means that he holds an image of you in an affectionate place deep within him. You are obviously not literally inside of him. When God holds you in His Heart, however, it is a literal thing. Your being is literally inside of God's Heart, inside His infinite Love. That is your home, and while sleeping there you simply dream of being somewhere else, in a world of time and space.

Finally, the gifts you have made for God are not things made with crayons, paper, and glue. They are the gifts of forgiveness you have given your brothers here in this world, gifts that relieved those brothers of the torturous burden of guilt they carried. They are gifts to God because they healed His beloved Son. By relieving the Son of guilt they, in a very real sense, "took him from the cross." And what parent wouldn't be grateful to someone who saved his son?

This passage, then, is an excellent window on how the earthly father-son relationship can be used to symbolize the divine Father-Son relationship. Let us go on to the next passage.

Sharing God's Name

> God's Name is holy, but no holier than yours. To call upon His Name is but to call upon your own. A father gives his son his name, and thus identifies the son with him. His brothers share his name, and thus are they united in a bond to which they turn for their identity. Your Father's Name reminds you who you are, even within a world that does not know; even though you have not remembered it. (W-pI.183.1:1-5)

This passage, of course, refers to the same phenomenon that we mentioned earlier: "A father gives his son his name, and thus identifies the son with him." This is such a basic part of the fabric of our world that we scarcely reflect on it. However, when we see this phenomenon as a symbol of our relationship with God, the results are profound. It means that just as an earthly father and son share the same surname, a name which stands for their shared identity, so we share the same Name with God. God's Name is also *our* Name. And this Name stands for our shared Identity with Him. This means that when we call upon God's Name, we are also calling upon our own. We are simultaneously calling on our true Identity. When we say "God," we are addressing both God *and* our own Self. In a world of forgetfulness, just thinking about God's Name reminds us of who we really are.

The loving father of the prodigal son

> Listen to the story of the prodigal son, and learn what God's treasure is and yours: This son of a loving father left his home and thought he had squandered everything for nothing of any value, although he had not understood its worthlessness at the time. He was ashamed to return to his father, because he thought he had hurt him. Yet when he came home the father welcomed him with joy, because the son himself *was* his father's treasure. He wanted nothing else.
>
> God wants only His Son because His Son is His only treasure.
>
> (T-8.VI.4:1–5:1)

The parable of the prodigal son is, interestingly, the only biblical parable that Jesus retells in the Course. One might well surmise that this is because this parable's themes are so close to themes the Course holds dear. In particular, the Course is intensely focused on the idea of loving fatherhood, and this parable is one of history's great and enduring images of the loving father. That image is actually heightened in this retelling, for here Jesus makes clear what is not explicit (though certainly implicit) in the original telling: The reason the father could so completely forgive the son for squandering his father's treasure is that "the son himself *was* his father's treasure." The father's treasure was not the inheritance, but the *inheritor*. As this version closes by saying, "He [the father] wanted nothing else." The physical treasure didn't matter. He wanted only his son.

The line immediately following the parable ("God wants only His Son....") applies the parable to our relationship with God. It says, in essence, *"This* is what your heavenly Father is like. He is not the wrathful God you may have been taught. He is like the loving father of this story. Just as the prodigal son was his father's treasure, so you are your Father's treasure. He wants only you." Think of the implications of this. If you are God's only treasure, how could anything ever get in the way of His Love for you? For something to get in the way, God would have to have some *other* treasure that you could squander or destroy, thus bringing on His wrath. But since you are His only treasure, He can only treasure you. When you seem to leave Him, He does not get angry nor vengeful. He just wants you, His treasure, back; no questions asked, no payment needed, no judgment required.

A father's gentle guidance

Lead our practicing as does a father lead a little child along a way he does not understand. Yet does he follow, sure that he is safe because his father leads the way for him.

So do we bring our practicing to You. And if we stumble, You will raise us up. If we forget the way, we count upon Your sure remembering. We wander off, but You will not forget to call us back. (W-pI.rV.In.2:5–3:4)

Here we have another image of a loving father. In this case, he is leading a very small child by the hand along a path. The child does not know where he is going nor how to get there. This could be a source of great fear and anxiety. Yet he feels perfectly safe, for his hand is in his father's.

Once again, the passage applies this image to our relationship with God. On the pathway home, it implies, we are just like the little child on his footpath. We stumble. We forget the way. We wander off. If we are honest with ourselves, we know that this is exactly our behavior on the spiritual path. And somewhere in our minds looms an image of how God responds. We see Him as keeping a judicious distance, either actively frowning on us or deliberately ignoring us, having decided we are not worthy of His efforts to help.

Yet the analogy of the loving father provides an entirely different picture. Just as any loving father would do, our Father walks beside us on the pathway home. He never keeps His distance, never frowns or ignores us. Instead, He conscientiously leads us, making sure we arrive safely at our destination. Therefore, if we stumble, He raises us up. "If we forget the way," we can depend on Him to remember for us. If we wander off the path, He will never forget to call us back. Imagine truly thinking this way as we blunder along on the spiritual path.

The understanding father

> We are forgiven now. And we are saved from all the wrath we thought belonged to God, and found it was a dream. We are restored to sanity, in which we understand that anger is insane, attack is mad, and vengeance merely foolish fantasy. We have been saved from wrath because we learned we were mistaken. Nothing more than that. And is a father angry at his son because he failed to understand the truth?
>
> We come in honesty to God and say we did not understand, and ask Him to help us to learn His lessons, through the Voice of His Own Teacher. Would He hurt His Son? Or would He rush to answer him, and say, "This is My Son, and all I have is his"? Be certain He will answer thus, for these are His Own Words to you. And more than that can no one ever have, for in these Words is all there is, and all that there will be throughout all time and in eternity. (W-pII.Final Lessons.In.5:2–6:5)

This is a wonderful passage. We thought that we had sinned. We believed that our anger, attack, and vengeance transformed us into guilty sinners who deserved God's wrath. Yet our animosity toward our brothers was not a sin. It was merely a mistake. We simply did not understand. "Nothing more than that." How would God respond to this? How would *any* loving father respond? The Course gives the obvious answer in the form of a rhetorical question: "And is a father angry at his son because he failed to understand the truth?"

Therefore, rather than fleeing God's wrath, we can come in honesty and innocence to Him "and say we did not understand, and ask Him to help us to learn His lessons." We may still suspect that God might respond to this by hurting us. But the response we actually get is the complete opposite. Like any truly loving father, He rushes to answer us, saying, "This is My Son, and all I have is his." (Indeed, this is what the prodigal son's father said to his eldest son: "All that is mine is yours.")

On the lips of an earthly father, these words mean a great deal. But coming from God, their meaning exceeds the scope of our comprehension. Imagine God saying to you personally, "You, [fill in your name], are My Son, and all I have is yours." Try to take this statement personally. The Course clearly wants you to do so, for it urges you, "Be certain He will answer thus," saying that "these are His Own Words to you." If you really take these words personally, you will understand why the final line says, "For in these Words is all there is, and all that there will be throughout all time and in eternity."

Perhaps now we can appreciate the power of using the loving father as a symbol for God. It says that we are the extension, completion, and continuation of God's Identity. As such, He loves us with everything He is. Out of this Love, He provides for our every need, placing us in an eternal state of grace in which everything is freely ours. Even when we reject Him and fall asleep to Him, He does not reject us. He goes on loving us with the same everlasting Love, and provides us with the constant care and guidance we need in order to wake up to Him. In the end, He gives us all that He has. He shares His Name with us. He passes on to us His function (of creating in Heaven). He makes His Kingdom our own. What could our response be but to love Him forever, with a love that we can fall asleep to, but can never change?

The symbol of the loving father does more than just *say* all of this about our relationship with God. Because the loving father is such a familiar and deeply imbedded image, it has the power to instill these truths deeply in our minds. It awakens in us an indescribable sense, a real feeling for this kind of loving relationship with our Creator.

A CORRECTION FOR THE TRADITIONAL LANGUAGE OF GOD THE FATHER AND GOD THE SON

As I hope the above has shown, the image of the father-son relationship is an excellent symbol for what the Course wants to say about our relationship with God. Yet it is only a symbol. Other symbols could have been used. One that leaps readily to mind is the mother-daughter relationship. Why didn't the Course use that one? Why, instead, did it use a traditional image that is full of negative connotations?

There are at least three negative connotations in the language of God the Father and God the Son. The first is the traditional concept that "the Son" refers exclusively to Jesus, God's "only begotten Son," according to the Gospel of John (John 3:16, for instance). According to this idea, the rest of us are not Sons of God by nature, but can become sons through our faith in Jesus Christ. The second negative connotation is that the Father-Son language suggests that God is literally masculine and that he favors the masculine; after all, look at his special relationship with His Son. If this language excludes all of humanity from being a genuine part of God's family, it excludes women even more. They become not second- but third-class citizens in the Kingdom of God. The third negative connotation comes simply from the idea of "father." Our usual associations are that a father is both caring and wrathful, attentive and remote, kind and stern. When we are *already* tempted to believe that God is wrathful, remote, and stern, who needs a word like "father" to confirm our worst fears?

We might understandably suspect that something went wrong in the Course's choice to use this traditional language. Perhaps the author was just careless; perhaps his scribe was somehow blocked. Perhaps the Course came through at the end of an era, before the use of masculine pronouns to indicate a person of either sex fell out of use, and if it were to be channeled today, the language would be different.

I do not think these explanations are adequate. My experience in studying the Course's use of language is that there is nothing careless nor erroneous about the terms the author chooses. Over and over, I can see that vast and loving wisdom went into every single term the Course employs. I believe its use of traditional Father-Son language is deliberate, and is actually just another instance of a pervasive method the Course employs in regard to many terms: It uses traditional forms yet fills them with new meaning. This reflects its larger teaching that the Holy Spirit uses all the forms we made, yet assigns to them a radically different purpose.

We would probably wish that the Course had invented new terms for the relationship between God and ourselves. Wouldn't that have been great? Yet the Course *never* invents new terms. It never even appropriates *foreign* terms; terms, for instance, from Hinduism and Buddhism that might be closer to its actual meaning. It uses familiar English terms, often Christian terms laden with centuries of emotional associations. Yet this does *not* imply a wholesale approval of the meaning of those terms. In fact, it implies just the opposite. It implies a rejection of some of the core meanings of those terms.

Just as the author of the Course is intimately familiar with all aspects of the human father-son relationship, so he is intensely familiar with all the pain wrought by traditional Christian terms. He knows they have caused generations of people to feel alienated, excluded, sinful, and afraid. And that is *why* he uses them. Were he to invent new terms, this would affirm that the old terms are just too dirty, too evil to be used by the Holy Spirit, and therefore they must really be sins. Thus, even while we delighted in his new terms, the old ones would still be sitting in our minds like festering wounds, dark and unhealed. They would be the enduring proof that the traditions that invented those terms really *did* victimize us.

Instead, the author of the Course takes the old terms, retains the meaning he likes, strips away the meanings he doesn't, and fills the empty spaces with profoundly different meaning. Let's take the three negative connotations of traditional Father-Son language and see how the Course corrects them.

First, in the Course, God's Son is not limited to Jesus. Rather, we are all God's Son. The Son is a limitless Self that includes within His boundless being all living minds, all of which are called Sons of God. And these Sons are not different selves that are somehow linked. They all share the exact same Self. They are all parts of the one Self, the one Son of God. And all the parts of this Self are perfectly equal, which means that we and Jesus are equals. Within this vast Self, we and Jesus are the same in every way.

Second, the terms Father and Son in the Course do not imply that God and His Son are males, not in the least. For the Course refers to everyone—men and women alike—as "he." Yet this "he" is no more masculine than feminine. The qualities ascribed to God and His Son include qualities both traditionally considered masculine and those considered feminine. Which brings us to one conclusion: The masculine pronoun in the Course actually refers to something that is gender-free. God and His Son have no gender. How could They? Gender is based upon bodies. Gender— one of the great separations in this world—is an illusion. It ulti- mately does not matter. It is unreal. Whether apparently male or seemingly female, "There is no difference among the Sons of God" (T-26.VII.19:5).

Third, as we saw earlier, the Course's image of "father" is not our usual image of someone both loving and angry, helpful and distant. The Course is exclusively using the one side, the loving. The Course, therefore, does not want us to project a conventional father image onto God. It wants to take the perfect father, the father of the prodigal son, and use him as a distant symbol of our real Father. It wants to employ this earthly symbol to suggest something beyond our current comprehension, to send our minds beyond the bounds of the conventional, toward a Love that is not of this universe.

At first, the Course's use of Father-Son language can bring up a lot of old issues. And, in my opinion, it is meant to. How else can they be healed? Slowly, though, a transformation occurs. The old meanings get brought to the surface, and there come face-to-face with the Course's new meanings. Gradually, the mind makes a shift from one to the other. As this shift occurs, the mind begins to associate the old terms with the *new* meanings. Now, when we read of God as "Father," we have a whole new set of mental and emotional responses. Before, we may have felt subtly excluded, outside of the fold, and afraid of God's fatherly rebuke. Now, we will know that His Son is not someone else, not some unique historical figure, not someone other than us. The feeling will wash over us that *we* are God's Son, His only treasure. We will feel Him saying to us, "This is My Son, and all I have is his." Gender will not be an issue, for we will realize that God is neither masculine nor feminine, and that neither are we. How can we be defensive about our gender when we don't have one? We will realize that the language of Father and Son is not literal, but is a beautiful symbol, an elevator that can lift us past the bottom floors of our thinking about God, and up through the roof into the open night sky. We will know in our hearts that our God is like a perfectly loving, understanding father—only expanded to infinity.

Perry & Watson

4

A GOD of LOVE

Robert

"GOD IS LOVE." These words from the New Testament (I John 4:16) are some of the most wonderful ever written. They have been quoted so often that they have become part of our cultural fund of knowledge. Almost everyone is familiar with these words.

These words are so enduring, I believe, because they speak to a yearning deep within the human heart. We yearn for a God Who is perfection itself, a God Who has no flaws whatsoever. We want a God we can love without reservation, a God who is not fearsome, but welcoming and inviting. We want a God Whose Nature reassures us that at the fount and core of reality is pure goodness. We want a God Who is shelter from the storm, not *bringer* of the storm. We want a God of Love.

The legacy of many traditional religions, both East and West, however, is a God Who is both Love and vengeance. He is both Creator and destroyer; Redeemer and judge. He thus has two sides to Him, and with these two sides He evokes an understandably mixed response from us. We both love and fear Him. We are attracted to Him yet keep our distance. We want to stand before Him and gaze on His glory, but fear we might get fried by His wrath.

I will be discussing the fearful side of the traditional God in Chapter 6. For now, I want to discuss the Course's vision of a loving God, for that is really the essence of its conception of God. It has completely stripped away the vengeful side of our notion of God and left only the loving. It has taken the New Testament proclamation that God is Love and fashioned an entire portrait of God from what is implied in those three simple words.

Since "God is Love" is the sum total of the Course's conception of God, this entire book is really about that single theme. In this chapter, however, my aim is to help that idea sink in. We have all heard that God is Love for ages, but has it really penetrated our minds? When we think about God do we habitually envision Him smiling on us, pouring out His Love upon us? Or do we picture Him frowning on us, or perhaps imagine His indifferent gaze turned elsewhere as He ignores us for more important matters? Chances are that our inner sense of God is at least somewhat tainted with the frowning or indifferent god. Therefore, in this chapter I will use various means to attempt to move that sense toward a God of pure Love.

GOD HAS NEVER CAUSED US SUFFERING

One of the real keys, I believe, to allowing in the idea of a loving God is to get it clear in our minds that God has never caused us suffering. In our usual concept, God has inflicted us with manifold pains, which clearly implies that He is cruel and fearful. If we are going to really accept a God of Love, we must correct this picture. I will attempt to do so in five steps.

1. God created us as perfect beings in a perfect environment, free from suffering.

In the Course's vision, God created us as pure spirit, perfect and limitless. As spirit, we are not made of cells and tissue. We are literally made of the substance of His Love. As Lesson 229 puts it, "Love, Which created me, is what I am." God not only created us out of His Love, He put us in the environment of His Love. He created us perfect, and then placed us in the perfect environment, His Own loving Mind. In this state, any kind of suffering or lack was inconceivable.

2. We tried to introduce suffering, but God did not let this attempt be real.

According to the Course, suffering was introduced not by God but by us, by our choice to separate. This choice initially took the form of asking for God to make us special, to single us out as His favorite Son. As the following passage says, God could not comply with this request, because it was actually (unbeknownst to us) a request for pain:

> To "single out" is to "make alone," and thus make lonely. God did not do this to you. Could He set you apart, knowing that your peace lies in His Oneness? He denied you only your request for pain, for suffering is not of His creation. Having given you creation, He could not take it from you. (T-13.III.12:1–5)

We were determined, however, to have our request, and so we went ahead and dreamed a dream in which we were special. But, for our own protection, God did not allow this dream to be more than a dream; He did not allow it to become real. If He had, the Course says, "you would have destroyed yourself" (T-8.VI.2:5).

3. God did not punish us; He merely sent His Answer to lift us back to happiness.

The above quote about God denying our request for specialness continues by saying, "He could but answer your insane request with a sane answer that would abide with you in your insanity. And this He did" (T-13.III.12:6–7). No punishment, no retribution, just loving Help. God sent the Holy Spirit into our dream, not to teach us how bad we were for choosing this dream, but to gently lift us out of its misery back into eternal joy. That is the Holy Spirit's only job.

4. We, not God, made this world of suffering and death.

It seems so natural to think of God as causing suffering because we live in a world of suffering, and He is supposed to be its creator. If God set the world in motion, then He is responsible for all of its endless misery; He is the architect of a system in which everything is born in pain, lives in pain, and dies in pain, in which everything is constantly singing the blues. I recently heard this comment about blues music: "Blues is a device for confronting the facts of life. The fact of life is that life is a low-down dirty shame that shouldn't happen to a dog." If you assume that God is in charge of life, then how can you possibly see Him as loving?

This is why the Course is so emphatic that we, not God, made this world. We built suffering and death into its very fabric, for suffering and death deliver the psychological message the world was made to deliver. What is that message? If you are constantly barraged by punishment from without, it is very hard not to internalize the message that *something is wrong with you.* Somewhere inside, you conclude that you must have done something to deserve all this punishment. You must be sinful, and life must be God's way of getting you back. We made the world, in other words, to frame God, to make Him look like the author of pain. We made the world to reinforce the ego's core message: You are sinful and God is fearful, so you'd better stay away from Him.

5. It is our resistance, not God, that causes any pain we experience on the spiritual journey.

Another piece of seeming evidence that God is unloving is how difficult and pain-filled the spiritual path can be. On the spiritual journey we often feel called upon to do things that seem beyond our strength and ability, and to sacrifice the things that formerly made us the most happy and secure. We do all of this because we have been promised joy, peace, and a life purpose. Yet the promises often appear to not come true. Hence, as we trudge along, stretched to our limit, weary, often penniless, emotionally starved from having "let go" so much of what we valued, and with the joy and the purpose that we were promised nowhere in sight, we can begin to harbor bitter resentment against God. He can begin to look like anything but a God of Love.

Yet, again, according to the Course, all of the pain comes from our side, from our resistance to His gentle leading. We are exactly like a recalcitrant piano student being taught by a master teacher. The student resists doing what her teacher says simply because she doesn't realize that doing so is in her own best interests. She balks at the idea of frequent practice because she doesn't realize how much joy skillful playing will bring. She can't understand why she has to practice scales and can't just move on to concertos. She feels that giving up the bad habits she has acquired in her piano playing is a terrible sacrifice, because she can't see how much they stand in her way. And then, when she doesn't do what her teacher says, doesn't practice, and doesn't give up her bad habits, she angrily wonders why the mastery her teacher promised hasn't come to pass.

Is it not possible that we are just like her; that our Teacher, God's Voice, has taught us perfectly, and that all of the difficulty has come from our own resistance?

• • •

The above five points, I believe, provide a plausible explanation for how all of our pain has been self-caused and how none of it has been caused by God. In light of them, I would like you to simply consider that their overall point might be true. Just consider that all of your suffering, in any form, has in no way been caused by God. Consider the possibility that all of it has been self-caused, and that while you were causing it, God was shining on you all of His Love and giving you all of His help, in whatever form was most exquisitely helpful to you in your fitful dream of private agony. What if all along, forever and ever, He has been the good guy, the perfect Father, wanting only your happiness, and you have been the one foolishly resisting?

I believe that in many ways the spiritual journey is simply a process of considering, with ever-increasing depth and honesty, this one stupendous possibility.

LETTING IT SINK IN THAT GOD IS LOVE

The suspicion that God is not entirely loving is deeply ingrained in our minds. Overturning it is no simple flick of a mental switch. How, then, are we going to do so? In the end, says the Course, we only fully overturn our fearful image of God when we have learned perfect forgiveness. Long before we reach that lofty goal, however, we can at least overturn it to the extent that, when we consciously think of God, we imagine Him loving us, not rejecting us.

For me personally, the single most effective tool in this regard has been the prayers in Part II of the Workbook. Those prayers are so soaked with the feeling that God is Love that one cannot help but soak in that feeling when praying them. The more time you spend with those prayers, the more that feeling becomes a part of you by osmosis. Allen will be writing about them in Chapter 12 so I will not elaborate on them here.

What I do want to stress is the simple idea of letting this thought sink in through repeated practice. The Course has many ways in which you can practice the thought that God loves you. Aside from the prayers in Part II of the Workbook, examples are to be found in Lessons 47, 50, 66, 67, 93, 99, 101, 102, 103, 105, 112, 116, 123, 125, 127, 157, 168, 169, 170, 183, 184, 188, 189, 191, 207, 209, and 219.

And you need not confine yourself to the practices given in the Workbook. A technique that I enjoy is to memorize a certain passage and simply repeat it to myself from time to time, perhaps even changing the wording from "you" to "I" so that it becomes very much like a Workbook lesson. Perhaps the most moving passage about the Love of God in the Course material comes in "The Gifts of God." Often considered Helen Schucman's last authentic scribing from Jesus, it is included in the back of the collection of her personal poetry, which is also entitled *The Gifts of God*. Below, I have taken this passage, changed it to read in the first person instead of the second, and separated it into four parts.

Rest could be mine because of what God is.
He loves me as a mother loves her child;
her only one, the only love she has, her all-in-all,
extension of herself, as much a part of her as breath itself.

He loves me as a brother loves his own;
born of one father, still as one in him,
and bonded with a seal that cannot break.

He loves me as a lover loves his own;
his chosen one, his joy, his very life,
the one he seeks when she has gone away,
and brings him peace again on her return.

He loves me as a father loves his son,
without whom would his self be incomplete,
whose immortality completes his own,
for in him [the son] is the chain of love
[from one generation to the next] complete—
a golden circle that will never end,
a song that will be sung throughout all time and afterwards,
and always will remain the deathless sound of loving and of love.
(adapted from *The Gifts of God*, p. 126)

My suggestion is that you really spend some time with this passage in the following way. When you begin one of the four images, superimpose that image onto God and yourself. Then read through each of the following phrases and feel each one existing between you and God.

For instance, when you begin the mother image, superimpose onto God the image of mother, perhaps your own mother or another mother that in your mind stands for the archetypal loving mother. Then superimpose onto yourself the image of child. Then feel each of the following phrases as it describes how this mother regards you. Feel this mother regarding you as "her only one." Then feel her regarding you as "the only love she has." Then feel her regarding you as "her all-in-all," and so on, all the while realizing that this mother stands for God and that God's Love for you is *like this*. Then do the same with the brother image. Then do it with the lover image. And finally with the father image. Then you may just want to start all over. And after you have gone through it again, and perhaps again, you may want to write it on a card and carry it with you wherever you go, pulling it out whenever you want to share a moment with God and feel some tiny inkling of His measureless Love for you.

5

God is the ONE SOURCE, Creator of ALL THAT IS

Allen

"CREATOR" IS AN IMPORTANT TITLE OF GOD THAT OCCURS 192 TIMES IN THE COURSE. The concept of God as Creator is central in the Course's thought system. It is at the root of our problem, because the "authority problem" is our ego's wish that we create ourselves. It is the foundation of God's Answer: We are the Son of God because God created us. The Course's non-dualism, its denial of the reality of sin and evil, and even the assertion that our will and God's are one, rest on the fact that God is Creator.

Salvation is nothing more than returning our minds to our Creator (T-10.I.4:1). In several places the Course even says that to escape from all suffering we need only to acknowledge God as our Creator, and to accept ourselves as He created us.

> If you will accept yourself as God created you, you will be incapable of suffering. Yet to do this you must acknowledge Him as your Creator. This is not because you will be punished otherwise. It is merely because your acknowledgment of your Father is the acknowledgment of yourself as you are. (T-10.V.9:5–8)

Heaven itself is simply the union of creation with its Creator (T-14.VIII.5:2). The process of salvation, then, can be seen simply as a progressive acknowledgment of God as Creator, and a diminishing belief in any other source for our creation.

In "The Obstacles to Peace" (T-19.IV), the last obstacle is the fear of God, which is, in one sense at least, our fear of acknowledging God as our Creator.

> What would you see without the fear of death? What would you feel and think if death held no attraction for you? Very simply, you would remember your Father. The Creator of life, the Source of everything that lives, the Father of the universe and of the universe of universes, and of everything that lies even beyond them would you remember. And as this memory rises in your mind, peace must still surmount a final obstacle, after which is salvation completed, and the Son of God entirely restored to sanity. For here your world *does* end.
>
> (T-19.IV(D).1:1–6)

What we remember when we pass the fear of death is, very simply, our "Father." That term is then expanded in a long description of what is implied by it: that God is Creator and Source of everything. He is the Source of the universe—that is, the totality of all that we can know that is real and has existence.

Beyond that, He is the Source of "the universe of universes." Science has speculated extensively on the existence of alternate universes. If such universes exist—and this passage seems to imply that they do—then the one God is their Creator. Not only so; the passage goes beyond even alternate universes to the inconceivable; it says that God is the Creator "of everything that lies even beyond" the universe of universes!

God, then, is the Creator of everything that is. Nothing exists that God has not created. That fact is another reason behind the Course's introductory summary: "Nothing real can be threatened.

Perry & Watson

Nothing unreal exists" (T-In.2:2–3). What would threaten God's creation, if God created everything that is? How could anything unreal exist, if all that exists was created by God? Would God create illusions? How could He, if what He creates is real by definition, and nothing He did not create exists?

This memory, this realization, is what lies at the end of our journey past the obstacles to peace. The "terrifying" fact of God's Creatorhood is what we have been trying to hide from, because its memory ends the ego illusion.

God Created Us; We Did Not Create Him

If acknowledging God as Creator is the gateway to salvation and freedom from all suffering, then—since we still suffer—we must believe something else. What might that be?

The Course teaches that we believe in an absurdity: We believe that we have, somehow, created ourselves.

The Authority Problem

This absurdity starts, according to "The Origins of Separation" (T-2.I.1:7–12), with a belief that we can change what God has created with our minds. Then, we believe that such changes can make what is perfect into something that is imperfect. Third, we come to believe that our very selves are included in the things that we can distort; we can distort *ourselves*. And that leads in the end to the belief that we can actually create ourselves; that we can make ourselves into something God did not create. We not only believe we *can* do this, we believe that we *have done* it.

If we can create ourselves then we have usurped the power of God. "All fear is ultimately reducible to the basic misperception that you have the ability to usurp the power of God" (T-2.I.4:1).

Conversely, if we could simply acknowledge God as our Creator, it would do away with the thought that we have somehow usurped the power of God. And this would undercut the basis for our belief in sin, thus ending our guilt and our fear!

All of our choices in life can be boiled down to a single choice: Is the ego my father, or is God? This is what the Course names "the authority problem," which is simply our problem with answering the question, "Who is my author?" In other words, who is my Creator?

> The authority problem is still the only source of conflict, because the ego was made out of the wish of God's Son to father Him. The ego, then, is nothing more than a delusional system in which you made your own father....It sounds insane....Yet that is its insane premise, which is carefully hidden in the dark cornerstone of its thought system. And either the ego, which you made, *is* your father, or its whole thought system will not stand.   (T-11.In.2:3-4,6-8)

The position of God as the sole Creator is crucial in the Course. Denial of God as Creator is at the root of the ego; it is "the dark cornerstone of its thought system." The root of the ego is a desire to deny God as our Creator, and to become, instead, the creator of God. The root of the ego is a conflict over authorship! If God is our author, the ego is not; settle that one question, and all our suffering ends. That is why the Course says:

> I have spoken of different symptoms, and at that level there is almost endless variation. There is, however, only one cause for all of them: the authority problem. This *is* "the root of all evil."
> (T-3.VI.7:1–3)

The "one inconceivable thought" (T-3.VI.7:5) is that God is not the Creator; that we have created ourselves. The whole ego thought system stems from that thought. This is why the Course can say that if we truly recognize that God created us—with all that it implies—the ego will be undone, and our minds will be totally transformed.

The ways in which we deny God as Creator may not be immediately evident to us. We are probably inclined to think, "I already believe that God created me." We are not aware of all the ways in which we deny that belief by our thoughts and actions. The Course tells us,

> And if you think that what you have made can tell you what you see and feel, and place your faith in its ability to do so, you are denying your Creator, and believing that you made yourself. For if you think the world you made has power to make you what it wills, you are confusing Son and Father; effect and Source. (T-21.II.11:4–5)

In simple terms, any way in which we see ourselves as *the effect* of the world is a denial of God as Creator. If we believe that something "outside" ourselves is threatening us or making us unhappy or causing us to lose our peace, we are, in that very thought, denying that God is our Creator.

Therefore He is "above" us. Awe is appropriate

One implication of all this is that *awe* is an appropriate response to God. He created us; we did not create Him. That is really the only fundamental difference between us and God.

> Yet in creation you are not in a reciprocal relation to God, since He created you but you did not create Him. I have already told you that only in this respect your creative power differs from His. (T-7.I.1:4–5)

Because God created us, and we did not create Him, we are "of a lesser order" (T-1.II.3:2) than God, and therefore awe and even worship is appropriate in relation to Him.

> A state of awe is worshipful, implying that one of a lesser order stands before his Creator. You are a perfect creation, and should experience awe only in the presence of the Creator of perfection. (T-1.II.3:2–3)

One of the ways we relate to God, then, is in awe and

worship, and the Course affirms that this is one appropriate manner of relating to God. We also relate to God in intimacy, and in union with Him, but we should not entirely omit awe. Just because awe and worship remind us of religions we have left behind is no reason to exclude this aspect of relationship from our interaction with God.

GOD AS SOURCE DETERMINES
THE NATURE OF ALL THINGS

God as Creator of all things determines the nature of reality. He defines what everything is. Everything is as God created it, and cannot be anything more, or less, than what He created it to be. This is a theme that is endlessly repeated in the Course, and is, in my estimation, the most significant conclusion to be drawn from the fact of God's Creatorhood.

I Am As God Created Me

Some of the clearest statements of this theme come in the series of Workbook lessons on the thought "I am as God created me." The statement is used as the main idea for the day three different times in the Workbook, in Lessons 94, 110, and 162. It also becomes the theme for *twenty entire days* in Lessons 201 to 220. And a closely related idea, "God is but Love, and therefore so am I," is the theme during another ten days of review. Obviously this idea, which is centered around the fact that God is our Creator, is very important in the Course's thought system. Somehow, knowing that God created us is supposed to become extremely important to us.

Actually the idea that we are as God created us is introduced in the Workbook in Lesson 93. There, we read this:

> Salvation requires the acceptance of but one thought;—you are
> as God created you, not what you made of yourself. (W-pI.93.7:1)

That is a truly powerful statement, and it helps to explain why the idea we are discussing is so important. To say, "I am as God created me," implies that "I am not what I have made of myself." You can see the negation of the authority problem here, the denial of the idea that we have, in some way, created ourselves or made ourselves.

What we are being told is that *this single idea* is enough for complete salvation. Lesson 94 makes it even more emphatic. If you still happen to be wondering if the idea that God created you is really all that important, the first paragraph of this lesson should end your doubts. Look closely at the list of things that come from accepting this single idea:

- It brings complete salvation.
- It makes all forms of temptation powerless.
- It renders the ego silent and entirely undone.
- It wipes away all the sights, sounds and ideas of this world.
- It not only brings salvation; it accomplishes or completes it.
- It restores our sanity.

If God created us sinless, we must still be sinless. If God created us whole and complete, we must still be whole and complete. If God created us eternal and changeless like Himself, we must still be eternal and changeless, unaffected by death or suffering or loss of any kind. If God created us wholly lovable and wholly loving, then we still are wholly lovable and wholly loving. We did not make ourselves.

To think otherwise — and we do think otherwise — means that we are denying our Source, asserting that something else has made us *other* than what God created. Accepting this one idea, that "I am as God created me," is our whole salvation from all our seeming miscreations.

Lesson 110 adds something to this — if you can imagine adding anything. It tells us that "This one thought would be enough to save you and the world, if you believed that it is true" (W-pI.110.1:2). Not just you: the world, too. Take a moment to read the first four paragraphs of this lesson, and allow yourself to appreciate the incredible list of benefits attributed to this single idea. Truly, it is "the birthplace of all miracles, the great restorer of the truth to the awareness of the world" (W-pI.110.5:2).

Knowing that God is our Creator is crucial; it is perhaps the most important thing we can know about God. Without a doubt, relating to God as Creator has *limitless* potential for transforming our minds and our lives. It is, as this lesson says, "all you need to let complete correction heal your mind" (W-pI.110.2:1).

The Course just can't say enough about this powerful idea. In Lesson 162, it returns to it with just as much fervency and passion:

I am as God created me.

This single thought, held firmly in the mind, would save the world....It will mean far more to you as you advance. These words are sacred *[this is one of the very few things besides God the Course refers to as sacred]*, for they are the words God gave in answer to the world you made. By them it disappears, and all things seen within its misty clouds and vaporous illusions vanish as these words are spoken. For they come from God.
(W-pI.162.Heading,1:1,3-6)

There are some absolutely incredible statements made here and in the following paragraph about these words and the idea they contain: "I am as God created me." These words are the words God gave in answer to the world we made. They *are* the correction. The world is not as we made it! *Everything* is as God created it. The world we made "disappears" through these simple words. These words *come from God.* That is the most direct assertion of divine inspiration possible: "They come from God."

Jesus says that these words are "the Word by which the Son became His Father's happiness, His Love and His completion" (W-pI.162.2:1). God's creative Will extended and brought us into being. Taking this word to heart means that we are proclaiming God as Creator, and honoring all creation as His.

He calls these words "the trumpet of awakening that sounds around the world" (W-pI.162.2:4). I don't think it would be possible, in light of the importance Jesus places on these words, to overemphasize them. I don't think it would be possible to repeat them too often, or to extol them too highly. They are, perhaps, the most important words in the Course: "I am as God created me." He really goes to extremes in lauding these words:

> The dead awaken in answer to its call. And those who live and hear this sound will never look on death. (W-pI.162.2:5–6)

God is our Creator, and nothing else is! When we begin to grasp just how significant a fact that is, we will think about it constantly, we will proclaim it from the housetops. It will liberate us from every evil dream we have ever dreamed. Listen, now, to how Jesus wants us to interact with these words and to use them:

> Holy indeed is he who makes these words his own; arising with them in his mind, recalling them throughout the day, at night bringing them with him as he goes to sleep. His dreams are happy and his rest secure, his safety certain and his body healed, because he sleeps and wakens with the truth before him always. He will save the world, because he gives the world what he receives each time he practices the words of truth.
> (W-pI.162.3:1–3)

That is what we need to do with this idea. Wake with it in our minds, recall it throughout the day, and bring it with us into sleep; Jesus wants us to sleep and waken with this truth before us always, to literally never forget it: "I am as God created me."

Ideas Leave Not Their Source

Another sentence that is repeated quite often in the Course (six times to be exact, in those exact words, and many more times in variations on them — see T-26.VII.4:7 and 13:2; W-pI.132.5:3

and 10:3; W-pI.156.1:3; W-pI.167.3:6) is "Ideas leave not their source." The first reference explains quite clearly what the sentence means:

> Ideas leave not their source, and their effects but seem to be apart from them. Ideas are of the mind. What is projected out, and seems to be external to the mind, is not outside at all, but an effect of what is in, and has not left its source. (T-26.VII.4:7–9)

This idea is applied, on the one hand, to our projections—the body, the world, and so on—and teaches us that there is literally nothing outside the mind. Mind, and thoughts in mind, are all there is. Ideas do not leave the mind, although they seem to. We are all very convinced of the external reality of things that are not part of us, and certainly not within our minds. But they *are* within our minds, and in fact have no other real existence.

It is on this basis that the Course teaches us that we are affected only by our thoughts. Ideas do not escape the mind, take on independent existence, and then turn around to attack us and have effects on us, becoming our cause.

Likewise, the same idea is applied to God's Thoughts. God's Ideas leave not their Source. The thoughts God thinks remain in His Mind forever; they do not leave His Mind, take on independent existence, and then turn around to attack Him in an attempt to dethrone Him. Yet that is *exactly* what the ego tells us that we—God's Thoughts—have done.

The ego's goal is ego autonomy, which is simply independent existence. "Ideas leave not their source" teaches that there is no such thing as independent existence; God's Thoughts cannot leave His Mind and become independent of Him.

If the words "I am as God created me" counteract the idea that we are what we have made of ourselves, these words, "Ideas leave not their source," tell us that, as God's Ideas, we have never left His Mind. The separation has not occurred. We have never become independent of Him. God has not left us, nor have we left God to go someplace else; there *is* no place else.

Here are a few of the applications of this idea in the Course itself, some paraphrased rather than quoted:

> Because ideas do not leave the mind, we were created as part of God, and "this must still be true." We are part of God because that is how we were created, and ideas do not leave their source. (see T-26.VII.13:2)

> So, then, since no idea can actually leave its source, to believe that ideas can leave their source is what opens the door to illusions. (see T-26.VII.13:5–6)

> The realization that we cannot have left God's Mind which thought us leads logically to another realization: "I walk with God in perfect holiness." We cannot be separate from our Source; we cannot walk the world alone. (see W-pI.156.1:5)

> Ideas leave not their source. The emphasis this course has placed on that idea is due to its centrality in our attempts to change your mind about yourself. It is the reason you can heal. It is the cause of healing. It is why you cannot die. Its truth established you as one with God. (W-pI.167.3:6–11)

This idea, according to the last passage above, is central in the Course's attempts to change our minds about ourselves. That is why it repeats it so often; that is why it urges us to think about its implications. The fact of our creation by God, the fact that He is our Source and that, as His Thoughts, we cannot leave His Mind, is the key to our healing! This is what heals us and enables us to heal. This is why we are eternal, why we cannot die. Because ideas leave not their source, we have been "established...as one with God."

There Is No Will but God's

Another thing that is implied by the fact that God is the sole Creator is that there is no will but God's. If He created everything by extending Himself, He also extended His Will, and what God created therefore shares His Will. There is no will that is apart from God or opposed to God.

This is not a secondary idea. In fact, in Lesson 72, we are told that it is the central thought toward which all the Workbook exercises are directed!

There is no will but God's.

> The idea for today can be regarded as the central thought toward which all our exercises are directed. God's is the only Will. When you have recognized this, you have recognized that your will is His. The belief that conflict is possible has gone. Peace has replaced the strange idea that you are torn by conflicting goals. As an expression of the Will of God, you have no goal but His. (W-pI.74.Heading,1:1-6)

If this is true, then God's Will is completely unopposed. There is no opposition to it. What we perceive as opposition to the will of God is something our mind is merely imagining; it is not real. That is true not only of opposition to God perceived as outside ourselves, it applies as well to opposition to His Will we perceive *within* ourselves.

My Will is God's

Because we were created as an extension of God's Will, the appearance of other goals or other wills must be an illusion. Our will is God's Will; our goal is God's goal. We are not independent beings being asked to submit to the external will of a powerful being, something imposed on us from outside. We are, instead, being asked to recognize that this Will that *seems* to be external to us is actually *our own will*. We are being asked only to "submit" to being ourselves, to being what we, by nature of creation, have always been.

The Workbook bases several of its prayers on the fact that there is no will but God's. The main emphasis of these prayers seems to be on how this fact makes us *safe*. Nothing can oppose God; therefore there is nothing to fear.

I am safe today because there is no will but God's. I can become afraid only when I believe there is another will. I try to attack only when I am afraid, and only when I try to attack can I believe that my eternal safety is threatened. Today I will recognize that all this has not occurred. I am safe because there is no will but God's. (W-pI.rII.87.3:2–6)

There is no will but Yours. And I am glad that nothing I imagine contradicts what You would have me be. It is Your Will that I be wholly safe, eternally at peace. And happily I share that Will which You, my Father, gave as part of me. (W-pII.328.2:1–4)

Non-duality: No Other Power

A corollary to the fact that God is the sole Creator is that there is no other power; there is nothing but God. God and His creations are all that exist. And, unless God is insane enough to create something that is His opposite, or His enemy, there can be no opposite nor enemy. This understanding (that God is the only power in the universe) is what is called, in philosophy, "non-dualism." Not two; One.

If creation is extension, the Creator must have extended Himself, and it is impossible that what is part of Him is totally unlike the rest. If sin is real, God must be at war with Himself. He must be split, and torn between good and evil; partly sane and partially insane. For He must have created what wills to destroy Him, and has the power to do so. Is it not easier to believe that you have been mistaken than to believe in this? (T-19.III.6:2–6)

Because of the fact that God creates by extending Himself, the Course teaches that there is no hell, no devil, no evil, and no sin. For such to exist, God would have had to create them! And God is not insane. As the Text points out, it is much easier to believe that our acceptance of the reality of sin and evil has been a mistake, than it is to believe that God created something that wills to destroy Him.

CONCLUSION

To acknowledge God as our Creator means to accept ourselves as He created us. Let us, then, return our minds to our Creator. Let us, with awe, recognize that He extended Himself *as us*, and that we remain as He created us. Let us rejoice that ideas leave not their source, and that we have never left His Mind. Let us see that any will that seems to oppose God, in others or in ourselves or in the world, is an illusion we have made. Let us give up the mad dream of independent existence, and once again, joyfully, take delight in our total and eternal dependence upon God.

> *Father, I was created in Your Mind, a holy Thought that*
> *   never left its home.*
> *I am forever Your Effect; and You forever and forever are*
> *   my Cause.*
> *As You created me I have remained.*
> *Where You established me I still abide.*
> *And all Your attributes abide in me, because it is Your*
> *   Will to have a Son so like his Cause that Cause and*
> *   Its Effect are indistinguishable.*
> *Let me know that I am an Effect of God, and so I have the*
> *   power to create like You.*

(W-pII.326.1:1–6)

6

The FEAR
of GOD

Robert

OUR FEAR OF GOD IS A PRINCIPAL FOCUS IN THE COURSE. Before Chapter 19 of the Text, it is only referred to in passing a handful of times. However, in Section IV of that chapter, "The Obstacles to Peace," the fear of God is given a lengthy treatment as the final obstacle, the core of the ego's system. After that, it is referred to in dozens of passages spanning the remainder of the Course. In this chapter, we will attempt to understand what this fear is all about and why it is so important.

TRADITIONAL IMAGES
OF A FEARFUL GOD

The Course sets out to correct traditional images of a fearful God. Therefore, it refers to these images again and again in its attempt to uproot them from our psyches. Such references help us form a picture of God the Course wants to dispel. Let's review several of them now.

The belief that God forced
Adam and Eve out of the Garden

> This kind of error [the belief that God asks for sacrifice as a form of retribution] is responsible for a host of related errors, including the belief that God rejected Adam and forced him out of the Garden of Eden. (T-3.I.3:9)

This passage is from the section "Atonement Without Sacrifice," in which Jesus, with great care and emphasis, refutes various biblical teachings that say that God punishes us, demanding sacrifice from us as payment of our debt to Him. This view that God demands sacrifice is particularly explicit in traditional religion, yet it haunts every spiritual seeker in one form or another. All of us are afraid that giving ourselves wholly to God means giving up some of our greatest sources of happiness.

One of the classic images of God's punishment, of course, is God kicking Adam and Eve out of the Garden of Eden. It is a harrowing scene. First, God proclaims a series of punishments He is assigning Eve and Adam, such as the pain of childbirth and the need to toil for food. Then He drives them out of the Garden. Finally, He places an angel with a flaming sword at the entrance, to make sure they cannot return. The Course flatly labels this belief an "error." Let us go on to the next passage.

The belief that God punished
Jesus for our sins

> I was not "punished" because *you* were bad. (T-3.I.2:10)

This passage comes from the same section as the previous one and refutes another one of those frightening biblical concepts. Here, Jesus rejects, in the most plain, straightforward language possible, the traditional idea that he was crucified as a punishment for the sins of mankind. This belief, which Jesus in the Course regards as totally insane, has profoundly shaped our view of God. The Christian West for centuries has had to grapple with a God Who would do such a thing to His Own Son.

The image of the Last Judgment

> The Last Judgment is one of the most threatening ideas in your thinking. (T-2.VIII.2:1)

Here is another frightening biblical image of God. The image of the Last Judgment has so fixed itself in our minds that the Course returns to it repeatedly in an attempt to correct it. The idea of the judgment of the dead has found its way into many religions. It is found in ancient Assyria, Egypt, India, China, Greece, Rome, Israel, and is a prominent idea in Christianity and Islam.

A common image of the Last Judgment is one in which you stand before God on His throne (with your knees probably knocking), while He looks up your name in a massive book and decides whether to allow you into Heaven or toss you into the lake of everlasting fire. Needless to say, the Course rejects such a view out of hand. Instead, it opts for a God Whose final judgment of every one of us will be this message of pure love: "You are still My holy Son, forever innocent, forever loving and forever loved, as limitless as your Creator, and completely changeless and forever pure. Therefore awaken and return to Me. I am your Father and you are My Son" (W-pII.10.5:1–3).

The belief that God is punishing us through the evils of the world

> ...your delusion of an angry god, whose fearful image you believe you see at work in all the evils of the world.
> (W-pI.153.7:3)

Vengeance is His. His great destroyer, death. And sickness, suffering and grievous loss become the lot of everyone on earth, which He abandoned to the devil's care, swearing He will deliver it no more. (S-3.IV.5:6–8)

Our view of a fearful God, of course, is not confined to isolated biblical events. Most of us, at one time or another, suspect that all the evils of the world—from sickness, to loss, to death—are sent from God to teach errant humanity a lesson. We fear that He is sending these tragedies to enact His vengeance on us. And our darkest fear of all—clearly expressed in New Testament teaching—is that God has made the devil the current ruler of the world. What a terrifying thought: that God is so fed up with us that "He abandoned [the world] to the devil's care, swearing He will deliver it no more."

The belief that God is keeping secret our reason for being here

God has no secrets. He does not lead you through a world of misery, waiting to tell you, at the journey's end, why He did this to you. (T-22.I.3:10–11)

This passage describes another pervasive human belief. We find ourselves plunked down on this earth, assaulted from every angle with problems to solve, challenges to surmount, and emotional wounds to nurse. We have no instruction manual on how to deal with these things. No one told us what we are doing here. One of the more obvious things to conclude is that God is keeping secrets. He put us here; He sent us on our tour through this battlefield. And only when it's all over, after it's too late, will He finally reveal "why He did this" to us. God, therefore, is analogous to a child torturing small animals. A friend of mine calls this the Marquis de Sade school of theology.

The belief that God's gifts
show up initially in the form of trial

You have been told that everything brings good that comes from God. And yet it seems as if this is not so. Good in disaster's form is difficult to credit in advance. Nor is there really sense in this idea.

> Why should the good appear in evil's form?...You seek to be content with sighing, and with "reasoning" you do not understand it now, but will some day. And then its meaning will be clear. This is not reason, for it is unjust, and clearly hints at punishment until the time of liberation is at hand. Given a change of purpose for the good, there is no reason for an interval in which disaster strikes, to be perceived as "good" some day but now in form of pain. (T-26.VIII.6:6–7:1,6-9)

This passage refers to a typical religious belief. We are taught that everything that comes from God is good. However, when something actually comes into our life that seems to be from God, it often appears initially in the form of disaster—some tragedy, crisis, pain in the neck, or thorn in our side. In the meantime, we are supposed to be thankful in advance. We should try to have faith that someday its true goodness will be apparent and it will all make sense to us. This, says the Course, clearly hints at a punitive god. Only a cruel god would behave in this way.

The belief that God created a world
in which everything dies

> In this perception of the universe as God created it [in which everything dies], it would be impossible to think of Him as loving. For who has decreed that all things pass away, ending in dust and disappointment and despair, can but be feared. He holds your little life in his hand but by a thread, ready to break it off without regret or care, perhaps today. Or if he waits, yet is the ending certain. Who loves such a god knows not of love.
> (M-27.2:1–5)

This final passage is particularly powerful. It draws out the implications of seeing God as creator of a world in which everything dies. Think about it: If God created this world, then He has not only decreed that everything ends in the grave, He also dangles your own life over this very grave. Perhaps He will drop you in today. Such a god cannot be loved, only feared. If you do love this god (as the passage closes by saying), you do not know what love is. Your love is like that of the abuse victim who "loves" her abuser.

WHERE DO THESE IMAGES COME FROM?

What a God! He kicks Adam and Eve out of paradise, crucifies His Own Son, punishes us by sending us the evils of the world, turns the world over to the rulership of the devil, sends us blessings in the form of disasters, decrees that our lives end in death—only after which will He tell us why He put us here, but not before pronouncing harsh judgment on the clueless life we led and sending us, most likely, to hell for eternity.

Where did these images of God come from? One thing is for sure: From the Course's standpoint they did not come from God. Every single one of the passages we just examined is an explicit or implicit refutation of these fearful images. The Course is determined to root out all of them from our mind, as we can see in this passage:

> Can you believe our Father really thinks this way? It is so essential that all such thinking be dispelled that we must be sure that nothing of this kind remains in your mind.   (T-3.I.2:8–9)

If these fearful depictions didn't come from God, where did they come from? We might be tempted to answer: From those old men who wrote the Scriptures and ran the Church. The Course, however, provides a different answer. These images, it teaches, are the projection of our collective unconscious fear of God. This unconscious fear extruded these images, like magma, into the minds of the Church Fathers, so that they in turn would pass these images on to the rest of us. And this would allow our unconscious fear of God to rise to the surface and haunt our waking lives. The Church didn't teach a fearful God to us; our own unconscious fears taught the Church.

We have already touched on the fear of God in Chapter 1. Yet we need to wrestle with it some more if we are to appreciate the full significance the Course accords to it. The Course sees all of us, like dormant volcanoes, sitting on a seething magma field composed of our fear of God. Because our fear is so terrifying, we have pushed it underground. Yet just as underground magma produces earthquakes, hot springs and other phenomena on the surface, so our fear of God rises up in forms we may not recognize as such. We saw in Chapter 1 that the martyr who loves God is really driven by a hidden belief that God is crucifying him. We also saw that the atheist is driven by a hidden belief that God has abandoned him. Both, in other words, are propelled by a looming image of a terrifying God.

This is also the case for everything in between; even if God seems like a non-issue to you, the fear of God is driving you. We saw in Chapter 1 that, as a defense against an underlying terror that God is at war with us, we submerge the war and act like it has gone away. So if you are unconcerned with God and He seems unconcerned with you, this is actually because you are defending against a down-deep fear that He will catch up with you.

You are afraid of God even if you are fervently trying to reach God in prayer and meditation yet He seems hopelessly buried beneath inner clouds of obscurity. *The Song of Prayer* says this about such a condition: "A vague and usually unstable sense of identification [with God] has generally been reached, but tends to be blurred by a deep-rooted sense of sin" (S-1.II.3:3). This passage is describing people on the lower rungs of the spiritual ladder, where most of us would rather not class ourselves. Yet, alas, the description fits. Most of us look within in prayer and meditation and have some dim sense that God is there, but our contact is definitely blurred. Blurred by what? "By a deep-rooted sense of sin." This sense of sin, as we will see, gives rise to a fear that God will punish us, and an accompanying recoil from contact with Him.

So, if you thought that you had no fear of God, or had let go of that fear, the Course would urge you to think again. Whether martyr, atheist, unconcerned agnostic, or fervent seeker, you are sitting on the exact same magma field as everyone else. Anything short of the permanent experience of perfect oneness with God is a symptom of the fear of God. Why? Because fear is the emotion of recoil. What we fear we recoil from. This recoil produces a sense of distance between ourselves and what we fear. According to the Course, this is the only reason we experience a sense of distance from God. We are not actually distant from Him; we are merely recoiling from Him in fear. And this recoil makes the One Who is closer than breathing appear to be remote and unreachable.

THE FEAR OF GOD'S VENGEANCE

The Course is abundantly clear on why we fear God. As most Course students have learned, it is because we believe we sinned. As a result, we feel guilty, believe we deserve punishment, and fear God as the dispenser of that punishment. The following passage from the Workbook powerfully describes this phenomenon:

> If sin is real, then punishment is just and cannot be escaped. Salvation thus cannot be purchased but through suffering. If sin is real, then happiness must be illusion, for they cannot both be true. The sinful warrant only death and pain, and it is this they ask for. For they know it waits for them, and it will seek them out and find them somewhere, sometime, in some form that evens the account they owe to God. They would escape Him in their fear. And yet He will pursue, and they can not escape.
>
> (W-pI.101.2:1-7)

According to this passage, belief in sin leads to the expectation of punishment from God. Only once we have paid our debt—in the form of pain and death—can we be reconciled with God; can we be saved. And so we understandably flee from God and His "salvation," for this is surely a case in which the cure is worse than the disease.

The above passage, I believe, is not just indulging itself in hyperbole in painting its graphic picture. Rather, it is describing a state of mind that exists in all of us. However, except in the rarest of moments we are unaware of this state. We don't remember our original separation from God, we aren't in touch with the vast majority of our guilt, and we have denied how truly terrified we are.

This leaves us in a quandary. The Course claims that our fear of God's vengeance governs our entire existence on this earth. This fear is the guiding principle behind conventional human life. It is the source of all our fears. Yet, by and large, we are not aware of it. What do we do when the claimed source of our fear and suffering is said to be hidden in our unconscious?

One thing we can do is look for evidence of it on the surface. We can look at what this fear does. One very important thing it does is give us leg irons on the spiritual path. Most of us generally feel that spiritual progress is gradual and hard-won. We just assume that there are real impediments in front of us. We feel like miners hacking a tunnel out of the living rock. Yet, according to the Course, there are no real impediments. It is, after all, "a journey without distance" (T-8.VI.9:7).

What really causes us to shuffle along the path at such a slow rate is our unconscious dread of what we are approaching. As an analogy, let's say you were in medical school. You want in the worst way to be a doctor. Yet underneath this conscious desire you have an unconscious fear: You are mortally afraid of feeling responsible for the death of a patient. Deep in your mind, this is what you associate with reaching your goal. Receiving your M.D. means having a patient's death on your hands. What would be the result of this hidden fear? You would probably find that you never perform quite as well in medical school as you had hoped. In countless ways you would subtly sabotage yourself. Yet because you are not aware of your fear, you would have no idea why you were not performing better. In fact, you would probably ascribe it all to how difficult were the demands of the school.

This is how we are on the spiritual path. We seem to try so hard and with such sincerity, yet, to our disappointment, we usually find ourselves more or less the same person, year-in and year-out. We suspect that the spiritual path is just too hard. Or that God is not holding up His end of the bargain. The real story, however, is that we are dragging our feet. We do so because we are afraid of all the sacrifices we think are required on this journey, all the goodies we have to leave behind. This notion of sacrifice hints at the real object of our fear, for only a cruel god would demand sacrifices. Yet this god is what we envision awaits us at the end of the journey. No wonder we drag our feet! No wonder our motivation seems lax and our excuses so many. We have an unconscious dread of reaching our goal. We associate coming face-to-face with God, not with the death of a patient, but with our own death. Somewhere deep inside we are fully convinced that to close the gap between ourselves and God is to be annihilated.

THE FEAR OF GOD'S LOVE

Our fear of God's vengeance, however, is not the bottom level of our fear. Below it lies a deeper fear, as the following passage suggests:

Loudly the ego tells you not to look inward, for if you do your eyes will light on sin, and God will strike you blind. This you believe, and so you do not look. Yet this is not the ego's hidden fear, nor yours who serve it. Loudly indeed the ego claims it is; too loudly and too often. For underneath this constant shout and frantic proclamation, the ego is not certain it is so. Beneath your fear to look within because of sin is yet another fear, and one which makes the ego tremble. (T-21.IV.2:3–8)

The first sentence in this passage refers to ideas we have already covered. When we look within and try to find our true nature (as in meditation), we are generally unsuccessful. Why? Because the ego tells us that we will look on our true sinfulness and contact God's vengeance. "Yet," this passage continues, "this is not the ego's hidden fear, *nor yours who serve it.*" It is not our bottom-most fear. We can rephrase the passage's final sentence in this way: Beneath your fear to look within because of God's punishment is yet another fear.

This other fear, ironically, is the fear of God's *Love*. Yet why on earth would we be afraid of God's Love? This is answered very simply. The ego's one motivation is to keep itself going, to keep itself alive as a belief in our minds. And awakening to God means waking up from the ego. Oneness with Him dispels our belief that we are an ego, a separate entity. In the dazzling radiance of God's Love, all separation vanishes. The ego disappears; it ceases to exist. The ego interprets this as death. And because we think we are an ego, *we do too.* Hence, on a very deep, visceral level, we associate union with God as the total annihilation of our identity.

It is crucial to the ego that it induce us to share its fear of God's Love, for we are the one holding the power. We have the power to choose to dive into God's Love and dispel the ego. And unless we fear God, that is exactly what we will do. To save its skin, therefore, the ego must give us a reason to fear God. Yet there is no good reason—God is only Love. No one in his right mind would fear a being of pure love. If we were ever fully aware that our true fear was of God's Love, we would abandon that fear immediately, for it would make no sense whatsoever.

How, then, does the ego give us a reason to fear God? It convinces us that we are sinful and that God is vengeful. It presents us with a counterfeit God. It places a bloody, grimacing mask over God's shining Face of Love. Then, as proof of its position, it points to all the evils of the world, especially death. It says, in essence, "Since God is the One in charge of the universe, He is obviously the Cause of all the tragic things that occur in this world. In causing these things He is evidently punishing you for your sins. He is whittling you down in preparation for His grand finale: your execution, followed by an eternity in hell. He is definitely to be feared."

This implies that in some deep place in our minds we (under the influence of the ego) do not truly fear God's punishment. In this place we are actually *attracted* to it, for the idea of this punishment keeps the ego alive. If we think we are being whipped by Him, we will make certain we keep our distance, and so will never meet that dreaded fate of disappearing into His Love.

This attraction to punishment from God, says the Course, is the driving force behind conventional human life. This, for instance, is why we attack other people; not for the rewards, but for the *punishments*. We attack so that deep down we will feel guilty, so that we will feel deserving of punishment, so that we will fear God's wrath, so that we will stay away from Him, so that our ego will stay in business. It all makes a twisted kind of sense. In this deep place, then, we are attracted to God's (fictitious) punishment *because* we desperately want a trumped-up reason to stay away from His Love.

This brings us to a final, sobering conclusion: Our traditional images of a vengeful God, our personal sense of distance from

God, and our fears that the spiritual path will demand sacrifice from us, are all a direct reaction to a single foundational knowing deep within us. At the core of our being we *know* that God is Love. And all of our mad fleeing from God is founded, ironically, on our primal recognition of this one fundamental Fact.

Perry & Watson

7

The Ego's Attack on God

Allen

THE WHOLE ILLUSION OF SEPARATION IS A "REACTION" TO
GOD. IT IS A NEGATIVE TO HIS POSITIVE. The separation is entire-
ly based upon God because it is a denial of God, a negation of
God and God's reality.

It may seem to many people that God is not necessary to the
practice of *A Course in Miracles*. It is possible to follow many of its
precepts without any belief in God at all. The Course material, in
fact, affirms that this is so:

> To be a teacher of God, it is not necessary to be religious or even
> to believe in God to any recognizable extent. It is necessary,
> however, to teach forgiveness rather than condemnation.
>
> (P-2.II.1:1–2)

And yet, to understand the real basis of forgiveness, to come
to the realization that all beings must be totally innocent because
they remain as God created them, God must enter into the picture. Without a perfect Creator, how could we believe in the total
innocence of all creation?

Likewise, to fully understand the problem we face and to be
able to perceive all attack as illusion, we need to recognize that all

of what we experience "apart from God" is somehow *an attack on God*, a denial or negation of what God is. Therefore, the remedy will ultimately take the form of a reaffirmation of and reunion with God, which places God squarely at the center of everything the Course has to say.

ALL ILLUSION IS DENIAL OF GOD

All illusion is a denial of God. Illusion defines itself entirely in relationship to truth; it asserts that what is true is *not* true, just as a vacuum is defined by the absence of any matter, or darkness is defined by the negation of light. Illusions, then, are shaped by reality; by what they assert to be true, they unintentionally define reality. You cannot describe darkness without any reference to light.

Illusions are reality's mirror opposite. This is why the Course tells us, "Your salvation lies in teaching the exact opposite of everything the ego believes" (T-6.III.4:1).

God, we have seen, is All That Is. He defines reality. Thus, every point in the ego's thought system of illusions can be seen as a negation of something about God. This is why, incidentally, the Course asserts that even our fear and denial can be translated by the Holy Spirit into "a positive affirmation of the belief that it masks" (T-12.I.9:7).

> Son of God, you have not sinned, but you have been much mistaken. Yet this can be corrected and God will help you, knowing that you could not sin against Him. You denied Him because you loved Him, knowing that if you recognized your love for Him, you could not deny Him. Your denial of Him therefore means that you love Him, and that you know He loves you. Remember that what you deny you must have once known. And if you accept denial, you can accept its undoing.
> (T-10.V.6:1–6)

This paragraph seems paradoxical at first, with lines like, "You denied Him because you loved Him." But it makes sense.

Our hearts contain an "intense and burning love of God" (T-13.III.2:8) placed there in our creation. That love impels us towards union with God. But we wanted independence. Therefore it was necessary to counteract that love, to offset it with a vehement denial of God. The very strength of our denial testifies to the depth of the love we are trying to overcome! Therefore, even our denial can be seen as an affirmation of God's Love, and of our love for Him.

We have to stop hiding our denial, to "accept denial," in order that the Holy Spirit can show us that our denial is proof of our love rather than proof of our guilt. Our denial of God means that we love Him. If we did not love Him so deeply we would not rebel so strongly! That realization is the undoing of denial. And that is why Jesus says, "If you accept denial, you can accept its undoing."

Our illusion of separation, our fear of God and oneness, and all of our misery, stem from our denial of God and our pursuit of specialness. This whole world and everything in it, as the Workbook says, was made out of attack on God (W-pII.3.2:1). We made the illusion of the world as a place where God could not enter, a place where we could act out the illusion of separateness and believe it to be real.

Everything within the illusion, then, has some kind of negative relationship to God. It is all about God—but it is denial of Him rather than affirmation. Death is our denial of God's Life. Our bodies are a parody of life, a sick parody—often literally sick. Special love is our sorry substitute for God's Love. The whole phenomenal universe is the ego's spastic recoil away from God, the "big bang" of denial of the divine.

The Ego Is At War With God

The ego is at war with God. That is made very clear in several places. As our understanding of the ego and its motives increases, we will come to understand that everything the ego does is just a skirmish in this war on God. The ego senses that "something" is a threat to its existence. God, and our Oneness with Him, are drawing us continually towards God; the ego senses that if we give in to this drawing, it will be the end of the ego. So it resists tooth and nail; it lies, it deceives us, it throws up smokescreens, it strives to make us afraid of God so that we will not respond to God's drawing power.

> Surely you realize the ego is at war with God. Certain it is it has no enemy. Yet just as certain is its fixed belief it has an enemy that it must overcome and will succeed. (T-23.I.1:7–9)

All the conflict we experience, both within our minds and with the world outside, is really nothing more than a reflection of the ego's war on God. The ego does not want us to realize it is at war with God, and so it disguises the conflict as conflict with ourselves, or conflict with someone else. But it is all the ego's war on God, a war that cannot be won. The ego stubbornly believes that God is its enemy, and that God can be defeated. And we get suckered into identifying with the ego in this war.

> Do you not realize a war against yourself would be a war on God? Is victory conceivable? And if it were, is this a victory that you would want? The death of God, if it were possible, would be your death. Is this a victory? The ego always marches to defeat, because it thinks that triumph over you is possible. And God thinks otherwise. This is no war; only the mad belief the Will of God can be attacked and overthrown. You may identify with this belief, but never will it be more than madness. And fear will reign in madness, and will seem to have replaced love there. This is the conflict's purpose. And to those who think that it is possible, the means seem real. (T-23.I.2:1–12)

We are at war with God. It isn't a war we can win. And even if we could win it, we are attacking our Source, so we would be annihilating ourselves along with Him. The purpose of the conflict is for the ego to replace God on His throne of the universe. The Course says that, deep within us, we know this is what we are doing, and that is why we are so profoundly guilty. And yet even this is not the true cause for guilt, since we can never, in reality, replace God on His throne; nothing has really happened, as the following passage makes clear:

> Seek not to appraise the worth of God's Son whom He created holy, for to do so is to evaluate his Father and judge against Him. And you *will* feel guilty for this imagined crime, which no one in this world or Heaven could possibly commit. The Holy Spirit teaches only that the "sin" of self-replacement on the throne of God is not a source of guilt. What cannot happen can have no effects to fear. (T-14.III.15:1–4)

Every time we judge against a brother, seeking to "appraise" his worth, we are judging against the One Who created him and his worth — God. When we do this we *will* feel guilty, even though "no one in this world or Heaven" could possibly attack God in reality. We *think* we have attacked God, and so we experience incredible guilt. This guilt is usually so intense that we immediately push it out of our conscious minds and project its cause onto something else. We blame the world, or see someone else as guilty. The truth is that even this "sin" of trying to usurp God's throne "is not a source of guilt." It can't happen, and so it cannot have any effects.

The Course's understanding explains so much! It explains why we feel this vague guilt. It explains why we are afraid of God and afraid of "being lost" in Oneness. It explains why we have guilt, and why we project guilt onto others. It even explains, as we will soon see, why we seek special relationships!

Special Relationships Are Really Attacks On God

> *The closer you look at the special relationship, the more apparent it becomes that it must foster guilt and therefore must imprison.*
> (T-16.VI.3:4)

The Course says we engage in special relationships in order to project our guilt. We need someone else to blame. Why do we try to make other people guilty? Is it really the other person we are attacking, or is there more to it?

> Very simply, the attempt to make guilty is always directed against God. For the ego would have you see Him, and Him alone, as guilty, leaving the Sonship open to attack and unprotected from it. (T-16.V.2:1–2)

We are trying to make one another guilty because, by condemning God's creations, we condemn the Creator. It is the ego attacking God, that's all. It is the ego trying to split us off from God by causing us to see Him as guilty, and therefore to be feared.

How do special relationships relate to the ego's attack on God?

> It is in the special relationship, born of the hidden wish for special love from God, that the ego's hatred triumphs. (T-16.V.4:1)

The special relationship is born of our wish for special love from God. God denied us that "gift," and so we are now trying to prove that we can meet our desire with another human being who will love us in a "special" way. Seeking for specialness through romantic relationships, then, is an expression of the ego's hatred of God.

> For the special relationship is the renunciation of the Love of God, and the attempt to secure for the self the specialness that He denied. It is essential to the preservation of the ego that you believe this specialness is not hell, but Heaven. For the ego would never have you see that separation could only be loss, being the one condition in which Heaven could not be.
> (T-16.V.4:2–4)

Separation, or being alone, different, and special, is "the one condition in which Heaven could not be." Yet that is what we are looking for in our relationships most of the time: someone who can make us feel different and special. This is a "renunciation of the Love of God." It is an attack on God. If I am married, and yet turn for emotional or physical satisfaction to another besides my partner, that is a betrayal and a declaration that what my partner offers is inadequate. In the same way, when God refuses to make us feel special and we turn elsewhere to get that, it is a rejection of God's true gifts. Heaven is the *absence* of separation and specialness, so in choosing those things in our relationships, we are choosing against Heaven. But the ego never lets us see that; we are convinced that to be loved in a special way *is* Heaven.

This, then, is why the ego seeks to engage us in special relationships. It is just another battle in its war on God, seeking unbridled expression of the ego. "If you perceived the special relationship as a triumph over God, would you want it?" (T-16.V.10:1).

This Entire World Is A War on God

What we are trying to see here is that everything we do in this world, limited in goals to this world, is part of a "total context," which is "the whole religion of separation" (T-16.V.10:3). It is all a war on God. It is the ego's war, not ours, and not God's; but when we identify with our ego, we are wholly caught up in this war.

Every time we seek only to meet our individual needs—our special needs—we are engaged in this war. Every time we seek our completion or our happiness in anything less than God, we are engaged in this war. All of the discussion about idols in the Course is a discussion of things we have set up to take the place of God. An idol can be a special love partner. An idol can be money, or fame, or physical possessions.

> The core of the separation illusion lies simply in the fantasy of destruction of love's meaning. And unless love's meaning is restored to you, you cannot know yourself who share its meaning. Separation is only the decision *not* to know yourself. This whole thought system is a carefully contrived learning experience, designed to lead away from truth and into fantasy.
>
> (T-16.V.15:1-4)

A "carefully contrived learning experience." The whole thing, this whole world, was "contrived" to lead us away from truth and to destroy the meaning of love; that is, to destroy God Himself. God is central in the ego's madness because He is the focal point of all its efforts to attack.

> Here is the self-made "savior," the "creator" who creates unlike the Father, and which made His Son like to itself and not like unto Him. His "special" sons are many, never one, each one in exile from himself, and Him of Whom they are a part. Nor do they love the Oneness Which created them as one with Him. They chose their specialness instead of Heaven and instead of peace, and wrapped it carefully in sin, to keep it "safe" from truth. (T-24.II.3:4–7)

It's easy to see in the above how the ego's entire thought system is the negation of God, the negation of His role as Creator, and the negation of His nature as Love. *All* illusions are a denial of God.

ILLUSIONS ARE THE EGO'S ATTEMPT TO MAKE US FEAR GOD

The ego, in every illusion it throws up, is trying to keep us away from God, to keep us from discovering our own completion, and to give us reason after reason to fear God and to stay away from Him. Guilt is one such weapon of the ego in keeping us away from God. The *Manual for Teachers* gives a vivid picture of how the ego uses guilt to turn us against God:

> A magic thought, by its mere presence, acknowledges a separation from God. It states, in the clearest form possible, that the mind which believes it has a separate will that can oppose the Will of God, also believes it can succeed. (M-17.5:3–4)

There we have the negation of the Will of God; the idea that we can somehow create independently of God. A magic thought is any belief we have that we can find satisfaction, health, happiness, or peace through anything except union with God. It is actually an assertion that our mind has a will that is separate from God's, and which can successfully oppose His Will.

The Birthplace of Guilt

Let's look at a section from the Manual that Robert discussed briefly in Chapter 1. It addresses one common objection, which is, "I don't feel as though my will is in opposition to God. I am not at war with God, and never believed I was." How can we be at war with God and yet be oblivious of it? The section I want to examine begins by explaining that the belief that our will can successfully oppose God's Will may be impossible, yet we do believe it:

> That this can hardly be a fact is obvious. Yet that it can be believed as fact is equally obvious. And herein lies the birthplace of guilt. (M-17.5:5–7)

When we set our will up as separate from God's, guilt is born. We have attacked God and we know it, although we may not be conscious of it. The whole thing is impossible; nevertheless, believing it to be true, we feel guilt. And to reverse the argument, *if you feel guilt, you must believe you have attacked God.*

> Who usurps the place of God and takes it for himself now has a deadly "enemy." And he must stand alone in his protection, and make himself a shield to keep him safe from fury that can never be abated, and vengeance that can never be satisfied. (M-17.5:8–9)

Seeing ourselves as usurping the place of God, we perceive God as our enemy, from Whom we need protection. We live in fear of God's fury and vengeance.

> How can this unfair battle be resolved? Its ending is inevitable, for its outcome must be death. (M-17.6:1–2)

The "unfair battle" is us against God; the "ending is

inevitable." We must die. As the Bible says, "The wages of sin is death" (Romans 6:23).

> How, then, can one believe in one's defenses? Magic again must
> help. (M-17.6:3–4)

If God is against us, how can we possibly believe *any* defenses will be enough? Magic thoughts, which involve our will in competition with God's, got us into the mess. And now, magic again tries to come to the rescue. Here is what "magic" tells us:

> Forget the battle. Accept it as a fact, and then forget it. Do not
> remember the impossible odds against you. Do not remember
> the immensity of the "enemy," and do not think about your
> frailty in comparison. (M-17.6:5–8)

This is exactly what we do. Unable to cope with the immensity of our "crime" and the realization of our inevitable punishment, we just *forget it*. "Eat, drink and be merry, for tomorrow we die." Don't think about it! Whatever you do, don't think about God!

> Accept your separation, but do not remember how it came
> about. (M-17.6:9)

This is how we got where we are! This is how most people live most of the time. We just accept the "fact" that we are separate from God and from each other, but we forget entirely how it came about; we forget how it was our attack on God that brought on the sense of separation.

> Believe that you have won it, but do not retain the slightest
> memory of Who your great "opponent" really is. Projecting
> your "forgetting" onto Him, it seems to you He has forgotten,
> too. (M-17.6:10–11)

So we end up projecting our "forgetting" onto God, and we believe that God has forgotten us. In fact we rather *hope* He has forgotten us, because if He hasn't, we are in really *serious* trouble.

We enter into a profound unconsciousness by choice. We have buried our belief that we have attacked God beneath a shield of forgetfulness.

> It is this quick forgetting of the part you play in making your "reality" that makes defenses seem to be beyond your own control. But what you have forgot can be remembered, given willingness to reconsider the decision which is doubly shielded by oblivion. Your not remembering is but the sign that this decision still remains in force, as far as your desires are concerned.
>
> (W-pI.136.5:1-3)

We do believe that we are at war with God, and the fact that we don't remember it most of the time is the proof that we still are choosing to block it from our minds.

Why We Get Upset By Other People's Egos

What follows here in the Manual goes beyond the point we are trying to make—that all our ego thoughts are disguised attacks on God, and that everything the ego is doing is trying to make us afraid of God. But it is so interesting, I don't want to miss the opportunity to talk about it. What follows is a description of why it is, that when *other people* engage in "magic thoughts"—for which we could substitute the phrase "anything that is trying to find completion in the world or by worldly means"—we get upset. Why do we get angry at a person who thinks he has to steal in order to have things? Why do we get angry at our friend who keeps getting trapped in co-dependent relationships? Why do we get mad when we see religious organizations becoming money-hungry? Why do we feel so judgmental towards someone who is addicted to alcohol or drugs?

> But what will now be your reaction to all magic thoughts? They can but reawaken sleeping guilt, which you have hidden but have not let go. Each one says clearly to your frightened mind, "You have usurped the place of God. Think not He has forgotten."
>
> (M-17.7:1-4)

I see someone else engaging in a "magic thought," and that awakens my "sleeping guilt." I think I have usurped God's place, and for that reason, my guilt has cosmic proportions. I have worked very hard, and have succeeded in large measure, at burying my guilt and forgetting about it. And then this dope comes along and does something my mind perceives to be sinful. Seeing him as guilty reminds me of my own guilt, which is exactly what I do *not* want to remember. When my guilt surfaces, I have a hard time convincing myself that God has forgotten my crimes.

When I get angry at my brother, it is not really because of what he has done, but because his guilt is reminding me of my own. It does not matter if the form of the magic thought in the other person is not a form I would choose; anything that reminds me of sleeping guilt and God's vengeance triggers my anger. This, of course, leads to my condemning my brother for his magic thoughts. And to condemning him for bringing up the conflict again in me. And to condemning him as a way of transferring my guilt to him. I become the righteous condemner of his sin, which makes me look clean and him look dirty. But underneath it all, it is a symptom of my hidden conflict with God.

> Here we have the fear of God most starkly represented. For in that thought has guilt already raised madness to the throne of God Himself. (M-17.7:5–6)

In other words, by attributing vengeance and fury to God, we have set madness on the throne; we have turned God into a madman.

> And now there is no hope. Except to kill. Here is salvation now. An angry father pursues his guilty son. Kill or be killed, for here alone is choice. Beyond this there is none, for what was done cannot be done without. The stain of blood can never be removed, and anyone who bears this stain on him must meet with death. (M-17.7:7–13)

The only response is "kill or be killed." God is after me. One of us must die; it's Him or me! I will most likely express my desire to kill God by lashing out at the person whose magic thought has stirred up my guilt. Perhaps I hope that if I can damn him, God will overlook me. Or, I may directly attack God Himself, thrusting Him out of my mind, turning myself away from the light in a vain attempt to hide from Him, or convincing myself that God does not exist.

How often do we realize in our reactions to other people's magic thoughts, which seem righteous and even spiritual, that we are reacting out of stark terror of God? How often, in righteously attacking or being angered by someone else's "crime," do we realize that we are attacking them only because we are driven by our own guilt, and are trying desperately to cover it up?

It may seem that we have wandered a bit afield from the ego's attack on God. But not really that far. We would not react this way to our brothers if we were not at war with God, and terrified of our omnipotent "enemy." We do not realize how completely this unconscious mental stance dominates all of our lives, our thoughts and our actions.

All illusion is a denial of God. All illusions are the ego's attempt to make us fear God. The entire world of dreams testifies to God because it is all a reaction against Him.

8

GOD the GOAL and the MEANS

Allen

IN THE COURSE, GOD IS LITERALLY EVERYTHING WE NEED. Salvation is in God, and God alone. That is why the ego's whole strategy is an attack on God, a denial of God, and an attempt to make us fear God so badly we want to stay as far away from Him as we possibly can.

Much of the Course's teaching on God is directed towards reminding us that God is both our ultimate goal, and also the means by which we go to the goal. The Course stresses God as our goal largely because the ego has taught us the exact opposite.

> Our Love awaits us as we go to Him, and walks beside us showing us the way. He fails in nothing. He the end we seek, and He the means by which we go to Him. (W-pII.302.2:1–3)

"Our Love" refers, of course, to God. God awaits us at the end of the journey. He is the goal. Yet He also "walks beside us showing us the way." He is both the end we seek and the means by which we reach that end. There is really nothing mysterious about this. God awaits us at the end of the journey and yet He walks with us, giving us the means to reach our goal. It is a fairly simple concept, and not that difficult to grasp; if God is God,

He can be everywhere at once. Indeed, He is everywhere at once—omnipresent. So even as we seem to be on a journey to Him, we are always with Him, and He is always with us.

And yet, although simple, this is an extremely important and practical idea. God is not distant from us. He does not *only* await us at the end of the journey, He is with us *now*, immanent, nearer than hands and feet. He is intimately involved with us. He is the very means by which we complete our journey. He shows us the way.

Some Course students seem to think of God only as the goal, and not as the means. Perhaps they see the means as only their own minds, or Jesus and the Course, or the Holy Spirit, rather than God the Father. But this lesson is clearly teaching us that God Himself is the means Who works closely with us in the process of our salvation. Let's look at this idea carefully. Is God actually with us, somehow, even in the dream we are having? Does He know we are here? Does He know we exist? We'll take a look at these questions in this chapter and the next.

GOD AS OUR GOAL

First, though, let's understand clearly the fact that God is our goal.

You are my goal, my Father. Only You.
Where would I go but Heaven? What could be a substitute for happiness? What gift could I prefer before the peace of God? What treasure would I seek and find and keep that can compare with my Identity? And would I rather live with fear than love?
(W-pII.287.Heading,1:1-5)

To have God as our goal means that the focus of our lives is towards God. To be with God, to draw near to God, to commune with God, and to reunite with God in full awareness is our supreme desire.

God is my Father, and His Son loves Him.

> *Father, I must return Your Love for me, for giving and receiving are the same, and You have given all Your Love to me. I must return it, for I want it mine in full awareness, blazing in my mind and keeping it within its kindly light, inviolate, beloved, with fear behind and only peace ahead. How still the way Your loving Son is led along to You!* (W-pII.225.Heading,1:1-3)

How can you love an impersonal force? How could you feel it in "full awareness, blazing" in your mind? The relationship between us and God is obviously meant to be one of *intense, blazing love*. The analogy of human romance is a pale one, and very imperfect, but the intensity of it, the way in which it can be a fire blazing in your breast, certainly parallels this love for God, and can help us catch a glimpse of the kind of fervent bond that is being talked about here between God and ourselves.

An old hymn speaks of this kind of love between God and mankind:

> *Teach me to love Thee as the angels love,*
> *One holy passion, filling all my frame,*
> *The bapt'sm of the Heav'n-descended Dove,*
> *My heart an altar, and Thy Love the flame.*

When I think of God as our goal, I tend to think of it in terms of a passion or a love. One of my favorite spiritual books while I was a fundamentalist Christian was called *The Pursuit of God*. The author, A. W. Tozer, quoted the Psalmist on the book's cover: "As the hart [meaning deer or antelope] panteth after the water brooks, so panteth my soul after Thee, O God. My soul thirsteth for God, for the living God" (Ps. 42:1–2). The entire book was about making our the pursuit of God our lifelong goal.

The Course follows in this same tradition:

> God is our only goal, our only Love. We have no aim but to remember Him.

Our goal is but to follow in the way that leads to You. We have no goal but this. What could we want but to remember You? What could we seek but our Identity? (W-pII.258.1:4–2:4)

And again:

What higher goal could there be for anyone than to learn to call upon God and hear His Answer? And what more transcendent aim can there be than to recall the way, the truth and the life, and to remember God? (P-1.In.2:2–3)

"To remember God" is our goal. The Course often mentions the return of the memory of God often as our goal.

What has been lost, to see the causeless not? And where is sacrifice, when *memory of God* has come to take the place of loss? What better way to close the little gap between illusions and reality than to allow the *memory of God* to flow across it, making it a bridge an instant will suffice to reach beyond? For God has closed it with Himself. *His memory* has not gone by, and left a stranded Son forever on a shore where he can glimpse another shore that he can never reach. (T-28.I.15:1–5, my emphasis)

"The Forgotten Song," the first section of Chapter 21, is a powerfully moving, poetic depiction of the memory of God as our goal. It speaks of an undefined longing that is in every heart, a wistful, patchy memory of something—something so wonderful that the merest hint of a memory of it brings tears to our eyes. It compares this to the memory of a song we heard long ago, in some wonderful setting.

The forgotten song, which we so dimly remember, is described as "this ancient hymn of love the Son of God sings to his Father still" (T-21.I.9:6). In Chapter 24, the Text speaks of it as "the melody that pours from God to you eternally in loving praise of what you are," and as "that vast song of honor and of love for what you are" (T-24.II.4:4–5). And Chapter 22 calls it "the hymn of praise to its Creator that every heart throughout the universe forever sings as one" (T-22.V.4:5).

One of the supplements to the Course is titled *The Song of Prayer,* and it refers to this same eternal hymn of love that is constantly exchanged between Father and Son. It describes the highest form of prayer as our fully entering in to this song. The goal within our dream is to return to the original state of creation, in which this song of loving union with God was all we knew. Participation in this endless joy and harmony and in the exchange of love is what creation is, how creation extends (see S-1.In.1:1–8).

God is our goal. We journey towards the day when we once again enter in to this song of creation with God.

As mystics of every spiritual tradition have told us, the attraction of God is our will; in other words, what all of us want, most deeply in our heart of hearts, is union with God. Our longing for God is the archetype of every longing we ever experience. In the holy instant, we hear God speak of His Love for us, and the longing of all our creations to be with us (or to be one with us), and we experience a powerful attraction. "It is your will to be in Heaven" (T-15.IX.5:3), and in the holy instant we are reconnecting with that will. We are experiencing the pull of the forgotten song, the deep, eternal desire to abide forever in God.

GOD AS THE MEANS TO THE GOAL

God is not only the goal, He is the means to the goal as well. "He the end we seek, and He the means by which we go to Him" (W-pII.302.2:3).

The Holy Spirit: The Bridge to God

We need to look a bit into the difficult subject of the relationship of God the Father to the Holy Spirit, because the key to understanding how God Himself is the means to our salvation lies in that relationship. I've used the analogy of a step-down transformer to help me understand the function of the Holy Spirit. A step-down transformer is an electrical device that can take input from a huge power source, perhaps 10,000 volts, and bring it down to the 220 or 120 volts that our normal electrical appliances can handle. To me, the Holy Spirit is somewhat like that; He transforms the infinite God into something I can handle. The Holy Spirit, in some sense, is not simply an agent of God in this world; He *is* God in this world. The following words from Lesson 47 show this near-identity of God and the Holy Spirit. They begin with an assertion:

> God is your safety in every circumstance. (W-pI.47.3:1)

How is God our safety in every circumstance? What follows answers the implicit question:

> His Voice speaks for Him in all situations and in every aspect of all situations, telling you exactly what to do to call upon His strength and His protection. There are no exceptions because God has no exceptions. And the Voice Which speaks for Him thinks as He does. (W-pI.47.3:2–4)

The Holy Spirit represents Him, stands in for Him as it were; God is our safety in the person of the Holy Spirit. The Holy Spirit is the formless that has somehow taken "form" in order to communicate in a world of form.

> He speaks for God and also for you, being joined with both. And therefore it is He Who proves them one. He seems to be a Voice, for in that form He speaks God's Word to you. He seems to be a Guide through a far country, for you need that form of help. *He seems to be whatever meets the needs you think you have.*
> (C-6.4:3–7, my emphasis)

The Holy Spirit takes the form of whatever meets the needs we think we have, even though He isn't fooled into believing those needs are real! The Holy Spirit is often called a "bridge" or "link" between God and us. There is a vast gulf between the formless God and this illusory world of form, but the Holy Spirit bridges that gap. He is called "the remaining communication link between God and His separated Sons" (C-6.3:1).

In order to fulfill this special function the Holy Spirit has assumed a dual function. He knows [an ability that exists only in Heaven, only in the realm of the absolute] because He is part of God; He perceives [an ability that exists only in a realm of duality and illusion] because He was sent to save humanity.

(C-3:2–3)

We broke communication, but through the Holy Spirit, God restores communication. He created the Holy Spirit as a communication link, to keep the communication going. Thus, *through the Holy Spirit*, we are still in communication with God.

The Holy Spirit is the "Voice for God"; God speaks to us through Him. This form (of a Voice, not a body) is not His reality (C-6.1:5), but it is a form He takes, because we need it. In the Holy Spirit, God, the Formless, takes form.

Does God work in this world? Yes, He does. God works *through the Holy Spirit*. This concept is repeated in each of the ten references from the Course we have assembled in Table I.

From these references, it seems quite clear. God reminds us; God speaks to us; He gives us lessons; He gives us faith; He establishes our function; He helps us learn our lessons; and He offers us miracles. And God does all of these things, in this world, through the Holy Spirit. There are many places in the Workbook where the lessons tell of things God does for us. In one very familiar passage in Lesson 72, we are told to pray to God and to ask Him to guide us very specifically in our daily lives:

Remembering this, let us devote the remainder of the extended practice periods to asking God to reveal His plan to us. Ask Him very specifically:

What would You have me do?
Where would You have me go?
What would You have me say, and to whom?

(W-pI.71.9:1–5)

GOD WORKS THROUGH THE HOLY SPIRIT

God, *through His Voice,* **reminds** you of it...   (T-9.VIII.10:3)

Through Him your Father **calls** His Son to remember.
(T-12.VI.4:8)

Listen to the Holy Spirit, and to God **through Him.** (T-14.V.1:10)

All this is safe within you, where the Holy Spirit shines. He shines not in division, but in the meeting place where **God,** united with His Son, **speaks** to His Son *through Him.*
(T-14.VIII.2:10–11)

It will come, being the lesson **God gives** you, *through the Teacher* He has appointed to translate time into eternity. Blessed is God's Teacher, Whose joy it is to teach God's holy Son his holiness.   (T-15.II.2:3–4)

Faith is the **gift of God,** *through Him* Whom God has given you.
(T-19.I.11:1)

Now hear **God speak to you,** *through Him* Who is His Voice and yours as well...   (T-30.II.3:3)

Thus, it must be that **your function is established** by God *through His Voice.*   (W-pI.66.8:1)

Listen, and hear your Father **speak** to you *through His appointed Voice,* Which silences the thunder of the meaningless, and shows the way to peace to those who cannot see. (W-pI.106.2:1)

Hear, holy Son of God, your Father **speak.** His **Voice** would give to you His holy **Word,** to spread across the world the tidings of salvation and the holy time of peace.   (W-pI.125.4:1–2)

For He would give to us the gift that **God has given** us *through Him* today.   (W-pI.198.13:3)

We come in honesty to God and say we did not understand, and ask Him to **help us to learn His lessons,** *through the Voice* of His Own Teacher.   (W-Final Lessons.In.6:1)

...**miracles, offered** the Son of God *through the Holy Spirit,* attune you to reality.   (T-13.VIII.7:2)

Does God, then, actually tell us what to do, where to go, and what to say? Yes, certainly He does; but He does so *through the Holy Spirit.* If we wonder why the Course makes this distinction, I think the answer can be found in this: It is a way of preserving the non-dual, formless nature of God, while allowing Him at the same time to somehow work within the world of form. In the Holy Spirit, God has bridged the gap between reality and illusions, so that, on the one hand, we would not be left forever stranded on a distant shore, with no way across the gap, and on the other hand, when we finally reach that other shore, the One Who awaits us there is unchanged and untouched because He has not adapted Himself to illusions.

This brings up the whole issue of the degree to which God actually participates in our process of salvation. If He is "ineffable," which means inexpressible, or undefinable, can we actually relate to Him? Many Course students, and some teachers, seem to think the answer is "No." God is so incredibly distant, so unutterably "Other," that we cannot, within this illusion, truly come into contact with Him. He is so wholly formless that He cannot be involved with form in any way. He is so totally pure and non-dualistic that He does not in any way impinge on this corrupt and dualistic world.

The section in the *Manual for Teachers* titled "Can God Be Reached Directly?" seems to give a very definite positive answer, but with a qualification:

> God indeed can be reached directly, for there is no distance between Him and His Son. His awareness is in everyone's memory, and His Word is written on everyone's heart. Yet this awareness and this memory can arise across the threshold of recognition only where all barriers to truth have been removed. In how many is this the case?   (M-26.1:1–4)

The idea here seems to be that while God can be reached directly, it requires a very pure mind and heart to have it happen.

Later in the section we are told that if we maintained a sustained awareness of direct communion with God, we could not remain in this world (M-26.3:8). So in this sense, it would seem that we cannot have much contact with God. But this does not take the Holy Spirit into consideration.

From the passages we have read from the Course, it seems quite clear that God does indeed act in this world, but not as absolute God, the Creator or Father; rather, God acts, God takes part in our salvation, *through the Holy Spirit*.

Through the Holy Spirit God receives our communication, hears our call, and receives the prayers of our heart. Through the Holy Spirit, God answers us, helps us, teaches and guides us, speaks to us and gives us His Word. *Through the Holy Spirit,* then, God is the means for our salvation.

> God can communicate only to the Holy Spirit in your mind, because only He shares the knowledge of what you are with God. And only the Holy Spirit can answer God for you, for only He knows what God is.   (T-14.IV.10:3–4)

GOD HEARS; GOD ANSWERS

What we return to, our goal, is total communication with God. If communication with God is the goal, then surely the path we follow towards that goal will involve increasing communication with Him. There is a long passage in Chapter 14 that teaches us this very thing. It begins with an admonition to ask the Holy Spirit to decide for us in everything, and it concludes, quite clearly, by saying that the whole purpose of leaving decisions to the Holy Spirit is to bring us back into communication with *our Creator,* or with God Himself.

> Say to the Holy Spirit only, "Decide for me," and it is done. For His decisions are reflections of what God knows about you, and in this light, error of any kind becomes impossible.
>
> (T-14.III.16:1–2)

We should ask the Holy Spirit to decide for us because, it says, His decisions reflect, or symbolize, "what God knows," which is our reality. A paragraph later, the passage speaks of our habit of not communicating with God:

> You taught yourself the most unnatural habit of not communicating with your Creator. Yet you remain in close communication with Him, and with everything that is within Him, as it is within yourself. Unlearn isolation through His loving guidance, and learn of all the happy communication that you have thrown away but could not lose. (T-14.III.18:1–3)

What can "His [God's] loving guidance" be, except the decisions the Holy Spirit is making for us? The guidance of the Holy Spirit is *His*—the Creator's—guidance. We have isolated ourselves from God. Now, through acquiring the habit of giving our decisions into the hands of the Holy Spirit, we are unlearning that isolation. The guidance of the Holy Spirit is the means given us to learn, or to remember, the eternal reality of our unbroken communication with God.

The section ends with this very intimate affirmation of being quite personally led by God Himself, through His Presence, the Holy Spirit, within us:

> Whenever you are in doubt what you should do, think of His Presence in you [that is, the Holy Spirit], and tell yourself this, and only this:
>
> *He leadeth me and knows the way, which I know not.*
> *Yet He will never keep from me what He would have me learn.*
> *And so I trust Him to communicate to me all that He knows for me.*
> *Then let Him teach you quietly how to perceive your guiltlessness,*
> *which is already there.* (T-14.III.19:1–5)

Let us all, then, seek to develop a deep and abiding trust in God to communicate to us all that He knows for us. Let us, day by day and hour by hour, open ourselves to His activity in our lives, leading us on the journey home, back to Himself.

9

Does GOD know we are HERE?

Robert

FOR A GREAT MANY COURSE STUDENTS IT HAS BECOME A
FUNDAMENTAL PRINCIPLE OF THE COURSE THAT GOD DOES NOT
KNOW WE ARE HERE, AND DOES NOT EVEN KNOW WE *THINK* WE
ARE HERE. Many quote the idea as a good thing, while many others wrestle with an idea they find to be very disturbing. If God
did not create the world (which the Course says plainly), and
does not even know about our experience of being here, the
implication is that we are all alone here. We can forget about the
divine cavalry showing up to rescue us. We can forget about God
even hearing our prayers, let alone answering them.

I heard this idea for so many years, and from so many Course
students, I began to wonder where exactly in the Course this was
said. Over time I noticed that it never was said directly. So I drew
conclusions based on inference. I decided that God knows that
we are dreaming, but does not know the details of our dream. In
fact, I had heard this very idea years earlier from Kenneth
Wapnick, who, I believe, is the source of the notion that God does
not know we are here. Ken used to teach (I don't know if he still
does) that God is like a parent who knows a child is having a

nightmare yet doesn't know what the nightmare is about. I still think this is roughly accurate, though it does not quite go far enough, as I will reveal later.

Yet I have found over time that making inferences from our general knowledge of the Course is just not good enough. We have to find specific passages in the Course that speak to an issue and see what exactly they say. Anything else is only guesswork. For the author's thought takes such surprising twists and turns that guessing what he would have said is a risky enterprise indeed.

So I finally did a little research into this issue in the Course and found a very consistent line of thought, one which, sure enough, I would have never guessed on my own. Apparently, Jesus was quite clear and consistent in his thinking on this topic. That consistent line of thought is what I would like to present in this chapter.

GOD KNOWS THAT WE BROKE COMMUNICATION WITH HIM AND ARE THEREFORE EXPERIENCING A LACK OF JOY

> Unless you take your part in the creation, [God's] joy is not complete because yours is incomplete. And this He does know. He knows it in His Own Being and its experience of His Son's experience. The constant going out of His Love is blocked when His channels are closed, and He is lonely when the minds He created do not communicate fully with Him.   (T-4.VII.6:4–7)

I have heard it said that this paragraph is metaphor, yet it comes about as close to a technical philosophical statement as the Course ever does. There are no flowery images here, but instead some very philosophic-sounding terms and ideas, about God's knowledge, His Being, blocked channels and experiencing the Son's experience.

This paragraph says something that is both important and surprising. It says that God knows our joy is incomplete. How?

This is the surprising part: *His Being is having an experience of our experience.* Therefore, He *knows* what we are experiencing. "Knowledge" is a technical term in the Course. It denotes a situation in which subject and object are one, so that my knowing of something is not a picture or representation of what I am trying to know; my knowing and the thing I am knowing are *one and the same.* And that is exactly how this passage reads. God's Being is having an experience of our incomplete joy, and this experience is not a *picture* of our incomplete joy; it *is* our incomplete joy. That is why the Course says, "His joy is not complete because yours is incomplete." If He is directly experiencing our state of mind, then our incomplete joy becomes His.

The final sentence of the paragraph describes the separation in two different ways: We closed off to His Love and we broke off communication with Him. We and God are like a married couple who are still in the same bed but have simply ceased to communicate. The separation was therefore not an actual physical parting, but a *communication breakdown.* This idea will gain importance as we proceed.

Let's now look at another paragraph which is closely related:

> You did not believe in your own perfection. Would God teach you that you had made a split mind, when He knows your mind only as whole? What God does know is that His communication channels are not open to Him, so that He cannot impart His joy and know that His children are wholly joyous. Giving His joy is an ongoing process, not in time but in eternity. God's extending outward, though not His completeness, is blocked when the Sonship does not communicate with Him as one. So He thought, "My children sleep and must be awakened." (T-6.V.1:3–8)

Just in case we thought that first paragraph was some kind of mistake, the Course repeats many of the same thoughts in this one. Here is a table of the similarities:

First Paragraph (T-4.VII.6)	**Second Paragraph** (T-6.V.1)
"And this He does know."	*"What God does know."*
"His channels are closed"	*"His communication channels are not open"*
"your [joy] is incomplete. And this He does know."	*"so that He cannot...know that His children are wholly joyous."*
"The constant going out of His Love."	*"Giving His joy is an ongoing process"*
"His Love is blocked...when the minds He created do not communicate fully with Him."	*"God's extending outward...is blocked when the Sonship does not communicate with Him"*

Both paragraphs state clearly that God "does know" something. They then go on to list many of the same things as what He knows. He knows that His children are not wholly joyous because they have broken communication with Him, because they have closed themselves off to the constant going out of His Love and joy. And He knows that this blocks His extension outward.

What He does *not* know, according to this paragraph, is that we actually split our minds. And why does He not know this? Because we didn't. God knows that our minds are still whole. If we could truly split our minds, then we would have overpowered God's Will. All we really did was erect an imaginary partition in our minds between our true knowledge and our illusions. This partition did not actually corrupt our nature, it just broke off communication. That is exactly what the Course says just a few lines before the above paragraph: "The separation was not a loss of perfection, but a failure in communication" (T-6.IV.12:5).

GOD DOES NOT UNDERSTAND OUR COMMUNICATION PROBLEM, BUT HE DID ESTABLISH A TWO-WAY COMMUNICATION LINK: THE HOLY SPIRIT

The Holy Spirit is God's attempt to free you of what He does not understand. And because of the Source of the attempt, it will succeed. The Holy Spirit asks you to respond as God does, for He would teach you what you do not understand. God would respond to every need, whatever form it takes. And so He keeps this channel open to receive His communication to you, and yours to Him. God does not understand your problem in communication, for He does not share it with you. It is only you who believe that it is understandable. The Holy Spirit knows that it is not understandable, and yet He understands it because you made it. (T-15.VIII.5:1-8)

We already saw that we broke off communication with God and that God knows we did so. However, though God is aware of our communication problem, the above passage tells us that He doesn't understand it. Still, He reaches out to this strange problem and attempts to free us of it. To solve our communication problem, He must communicate with us. And so He established a channel through which communication can still take place — the Holy Spirit. This is why the Holy Spirit is called the "communication link."

In short, we broke off communication with God, but God established a channel through which some communication could still take place. Note that this is a *two-way* communication link. It receives "His communication to you, and yours to Him." Like a telephone line, He passes on communication going both ways. We will return to this theme later.

GOD CANNOT COMMUNICATE DIRECTLY WITH OUR SEPARATED MIND, ONLY INDIRECTLY THROUGH THE HOLY SPIRIT

The guiltless and the guilty are totally incapable of understanding one another. Each perceives the other as like himself, making both unable to communicate, because each sees the other unlike the way he sees himself. God can communicate only to the Holy Spirit in your mind, because only He shares the knowledge of what you are with God. And only the Holy Spirit can answer God for you, for only He knows what God is. Everything else that you have placed within your mind cannot exist, for what is not in communication with the Mind of God has never been. Communication with God is life. Nothing without it is at all. (T-14.IV.10:1-7)

Why can't God just communicate directly to our mind in its current state? This paragraph gives an answer. It says that for communication to take place, the sender's message must see the receiver as the receiver sees himself. It then applies this principle to our communication with God. We assume that God is just like us, so we address Him as a guilty, attacking separate entity. Most traditional prayers are good examples of this. God, on the other hand, knows that we are just like Him so He addresses us as a guiltless, formless spirit. Upon receiving these communications, it is inevitable that each side will essentially respond with, "You must have the wrong guy. I don't know who you are talking to."

This is another picture of the communication failure between God and ourselves. The remedy, once again, is the Holy Spirit. The Holy Spirit receives God's communication to us because He sees us in the same way God's communication does—as guiltless. And the Holy Spirit sends our communications to God for us, because only He can address them to the real God, the guiltless God. Once again, the Holy Spirit is a two-way communication channel. But what does this two-way communication mean in more concrete terms?

THE HOLY SPIRIT TRANSLATES GOD'S FORMLESS CALL TO AWAKEN INTO SPECIFIC FORMS WE CAN UNDERSTAND

The Course is pretty clear on one side of this two-way communication. God issues to us a single Call to awaken. This single call is then translated by the Holy Spirit into specific forms that we can understand. He translates the law of creation into the law of perception. He translates formless love into forgiveness. He translates extension in Heaven into healing on earth. He translates God's Word into specific words that we can understand (such as the words of the Course). He translates the truth of timeless oneness into teaching that "takes note of time and place as if they were discrete" (T-25.I.7:1).

This idea of a unified answer that can yet adapt itself to multiple needs and thereby become countless little answers, is perfectly captured in this passage from *The Song of Prayer*:

> The form of the answer, if given by God, will suit your need as you see it. This is merely an echo of the reply of His Voice. The real sound is always a song of thanksgiving and of love.
>
> You cannot, then, ask for the echo. It is the song that is the gift. Along with it come the overtones, the harmonics, the echoes, but these are secondary. ...God answers only for eternity. But still all little answers are contained in this.
>
> (S-1.I.2:7–3:3,4:7–8)

THE HOLY SPIRIT TRANSLATES EVERYTHING WE EXPERIENCE HERE INTO A FORMLESS CALL FOR HELP THAT GOD CAN UNDERSTAND

So what about the other side of the two-way communication—from us to God? The Course says less about this, but I don't think the issue needs to remain a mystery. If the Holy Spirit translates God's formless Call into specific forms that we can understand, we might expect that our communication to God works exactly in the reverse. We might infer that He takes our many specific calls to God and translates them into a single, formless call. In fact, what reaches God would *have* to be something stripped of all specific form, since "God knows not form" (T-30.III.4:5).

There is some support in the Course for this idea. The *Manual for Teachers* says this:

> What you ask for you receive. But this refers to the prayer of the heart, not to the words you use in praying. Sometimes the words and the prayer are contradictory; sometimes they agree. It does not matter. God does not understand words.
>
> (M-21.1:3–7)

The implication of this passage is that God answers your prayer, but this does not mean your *words*. Instead, He hears and answers "the prayer of the heart," which (the next paragraph tells us) does not ask for concrete things but for "some kind of experience" (2:5). Thus, God hears neither our words, nor our requests for concrete things, but our heart as it reaches out for experience. This, however, raises a question: If we desire *egoic* experiences, is that the prayer that God hears and answers? This is addressed a few sections later:

> Never forget that the Holy Spirit does not depend on your words. He understands the requests of your heart, and answers them. Does this mean that, while attack remains attractive to you, He will respond with evil? Hardly! For God has given Him the power to translate your prayers of the heart into His language. He understands that an attack is a call for help. And He responds with help accordingly. God would be cruel if He let your words replace His Own. (M-29.6:1–8)

Here it says that the Holy Spirit takes our desires, regardless of their nature, and translates them into His language. Therefore, even our desire for attack becomes translated into a call for help. We find this same idea in the Text:

> Yet to the One Who sends forth miracles to bless the world, a tiny stab of pain, a little worldly pleasure, and the throes of death itself are but a single sound; a call for healing, and a plaintive cry for help within a world of misery. (T-27.VI.6:6)

Here we see that the Holy Spirit is taking not just our intentional prayers to God, but literally everything we feel—our pain, our pleasure and even our death—stripping away all the differences and particulars, and reducing it all to its pure essence: a call for help.

I think we can safely assume that this is what God hears. All that we experience here, all of our desires and thoughts, our pain and yearning, our particular situations and circumstances, all of it becomes boiled down to its irreducible essence. The entire human condition becomes translated into a single, pure call for help; or as the Course puts it elsewhere, a call for love. And that is what God hears, a call that says we feel incomplete here and desire His help so that we can know again His Love.

We could even say that God not only hears this call, He knows it. For the above ideas bring us full circle to the passage we began with. There we said that God is directly aware of our essential state of mind here, which is a lack of joy. Just now we said that God is directly aware of the essence of our experience here, which is a call for love. And since our call for love stems from our *lack* of love, both of these ideas add up to the same thing: God is aware of the pure essence of our separated state of mind — our lack of love, our lack of joy. He is aware of His children's state of feeling incomplete.

SUMMARY

Now let's string our different conclusions together so that we can see the whole picture:

- God knows that we broke communication with Him and are therefore experiencing a lack of joy.

- God does not understand our communication problem, but He did establish a two-way communication link: the Holy Spirit.

- God cannot communicate directly with our separated mind, only indirectly through the Holy Spirit.

- The Holy Spirit translates God's formless Call to awaken into specific forms we can understand.

- The Holy Spirit translates everything we experience here into a formless call for help that God can understand.

In the beginning of this chapter I mentioned that the Course displays a very consistent train of thought on the subject of what

God knows about the separation. Now we can see what this train of thought is. It all revolves around *communication.* We, God's communication channels, broke off communication with Him. He knew this and so re-established *partial* communication so that we could eventually be restored to *total* communication. This partial communication takes place through the Holy Spirit, "the remaining communication link between God and His separated Sons" (C-6.3:1).

This re-establishment of partial communication is crucial. If God did not know about the communication breakdown and did not establish an interim communication link, then communication would have broken down entirely. At that point, in some sense, we really would be all alone, cut off. We would be out in the cold, with no way to come back in. For the remaining communication from God is what talks us in from our aloof isolation. Without it the separation would continue forever, and, being eternal, would have become truly *real.*

Therefore, we have reason to be comforted by the ideas in this chapter. Who wants to be cut off from God? Imagine that you are apart from the one you love. Now imagine two different scenarios. In one, communication has been cut off completely. In the other, you have access to your love, you can talk on the phone or exchange letters. Some communication can flow back and forth. Who would not prefer the second scenario? God set up a communication link for this very reason: so that He can still communicate with us and we can still communicate with Him. Some communication can flow back and forth. He *does* hear our call to Him—a call that arises from everything we experience here—and He *does* answer us. The Course says that this is a promise: "For God has promised He will hear my call, and answer me Himself" (W-pII.327.1:2).

To return, then, to our beginning question: Does God know that we are here? Strictly speaking, no, because we are *not* here.

We are at home in His Mind, merely dreaming that we are here. Does He know that we are dreaming? Absolutely. His knowledge, in fact, goes beyond sitting beside us and seeing that we are having a nightmare. Instead, He experiences the essence of our dream. He feels the incomplete joy that is the substance of our nightmare—and it becomes *His* incomplete joy. He hears the call for love that is the core of our nightmare. Does He know that we are dreaming we are here *on earth?* He does not know the particulars, for particulars of any kind are foreign to His Mind. It is the Holy Spirit's job to know the particulars. But God knows what is *essential,* for He knows the *essence.* He is aware that we experience ourselves cut off from His joy, closed off to His Love. "And this He does know. He knows it in His Own Being and its experience of His Son's experience."

10

GOD walks with YOU

Robert

PROBABLY WHAT MOST PEOPLE WANT TO KNOW FROM A BOOK ABOUT GOD IS HOW WE SHOULD RELATE TO GOD RIGHT NOW. Do we conceive of Him as near or far? Do we pray to Him? Do we have some kind of active relationship with Him? Our final four chapters will address these important issues.

In this chapter we will discuss the notion of God walking with us, being near us, beside us, surrounding us. The idea that God walks with us may not sound like a very Course-like idea. Many Course students, in fact, would not think of it as part of the Course, believing that it sounds more like old-fashioned Sunday school than a radical, non-dualistic spiritual teaching: "He walks with me and He talks with me," as the Gospel song, "In the Garden," proclaims.

Why does it not seem Course-like? The idea simply sounds so dualistic. If God is really here with us, then He has apparently inserted Himself into physical space and is actually walking around inside of it—on invisible legs no less. And if God has actually entered the world of space and form, then that world must be real. The Course, however, is absolutely clear that the world is an illusion. We reason, therefore, that the idea of God walking with us must *not* be part of the Course's teaching, for it violates the Course's metaphysical foundation. It makes the world real. Instead, the Course must really teach that God is removed from our existence here, uninvolved in this world. How else could it be if this world is not real?

Yet are we really in a position to make such an evaluation by ourselves? Shouldn't we find out what the author of the Course thinks about this matter? Wouldn't he be the one to consult about what violates the metaphysical foundation he laid out? Thankfully, Jesus comments quite directly on the relationship between God being with us and the Course's metaphysical foundation. His comments occur in one of the main Workbook lessons to stress the idea of God walking with us: Lesson 156, "I walk with God in perfect holiness." This lesson suggests that we should ask ourselves a thousand times a day (which amounts to once a minute), "Who walks with me?" The answer, of course, is God.

Here are Jesus' comments in that lesson about how God walking with us relates to the Course's metaphysical foundation:

> It [today's idea: "I walk with God in perfect holiness"] follows surely from the basic thought so often mentioned in the text; ideas leave not their source. If this be true, how can you be apart from God? How could you walk the world alone and separate from your Source?
> We are not inconsistent in the thoughts that we present in our curriculum. Truth must be true throughout, if it be true. It cannot contradict itself, nor be in parts uncertain and in others sure. You cannot walk the world apart from God, because you could not be without Him. He is what your life is. Where you are He is. There is one life. That life you share with Him. Nothing can be apart from Him and live.   (W-pI.156.1:3–2:9)

Here, Jesus seems to be addressing our suspicion that God walking with us is inconsistent with the Course's metaphysical foundation. To say that he addresses it, however, is a little weak.

In point of fact, he *refutes* it. He makes a point of saying that this idea *is* consistent with the Course's foundational concepts. He says that God walking with us "follows surely" from one of the most foundational concepts *in* the Course: "Ideas leave not their source." A brief argument follows, which can be rephrased in this way:

> *Ideas leave not their source.*
> *You are an idea whose Source is God.*
> *You therefore cannot leave (or be apart from) God.*
> *Thus, "Where you are He is."*
> *Hence, if you walk the world, then God walks the world with you.*

This passage then elaborates on the argument, saying that you could never be apart from God because "He is what your life is....Nothing can be apart from Him and live." Now, as we will see later, the idea that we cannot be apart from God also means that we cannot *really* be in this world; we are still in God. However, its meaning in this lesson, with its focus on God walking with us, is the other side of the coin: God is *in some sense* present with us in this world.

What a fascinating reversal. On our own, we might assume that God must be removed from our lives in this world, and that the notion of Him walking with us violates the Course's metaphysical foundation. Yet the passage we have just examined completely reverses things. It says that God walking with us is not a violation of the Course's metaphysical foundation; it is an *extension* of it. It follows directly from the core idea that we could never succeed in separating ourselves from God.

Instead, what violates the Course's foundation is *our* notion of the true Course position: the idea of God being remote from us here. For if God truly was remote, then we actually would have succeeded in separating ourselves from Him. *The separation would have occurred.* That is not only the conceptual implication of picturing God as remote and removed, it is also the emotional impact. When you think, "Well, God can't be here beside me because the world is not real," aren't you left with the sense that a vast gulf exists between you and Him?

All of this reminds me of the section in the Manual, "How is Peace Possible in this World?" which concludes by saying,

> Now is the question different. It is no longer, "Can peace be possible in this world?" but instead, "Is it not impossible that peace be absent here?" (M-11.4:11–12)

In this same way, the question is not, "Is it possible for God to be present in this world?" It is rather, "Is it not impossible that God be absent here?"

HOW CAN GOD ACTUALLY WALK WITH US?

Yet we have still not answered our original question: How can God be with us in an unreal world? I have two answers to that. First, imagine that you are in a sunny meadow filled with a soft breeze. You, however, are psychotic and are so lost in a hallucination that you are not aware of your true surroundings, nor even of your body. Instead, you are hallucinating a scene in which you are an animal alone in a dark jungle. However, even though you do not see the meadow, it is still with you in a very real sense, and so is the breeze. Even though you are not aware of your body, it is still very close to you.

So it is with God. In this metaphor, the meadow, the breeze, and your body all are symbols for God. In Heaven, God is the environment we live in, the "atmosphere" that surrounds us, and the substance of our being. And we are in Heaven this moment, merely dreaming that we are human beings in this world. So God is still near us in a very real way, just as the meadow, the breeze, and the body are still close to the psychotic person. As the Course

Perry & Watson

says, God "speaks from nearer than your heart to you. His Voice is closer than your hand" (W-pI.125.7:2–3).

Second, as Allen discussed in Chapter 8, God is present with us in a very specific way through His Voice, the Holy Spirit. Walking with us suggests more than simply being near us and surrounding us. Space is near us and surrounds us (at least, surrounds our bodies), but we would never say that space *walks with us*. Walking with us implies actively deciding to be our companion on a journey, to take the journey with us and talk with us along the way. We could not say that God *as God* does this, for this implies an awareness of the specific details of our journey, and I do not believe that God has that awareness. But He does walk with us *through* the Holy Spirit, Who is aware of our specific journey and Who does take that journey with us.

We can see both of these levels in this passage from Lesson 222, "God is with me. I live and move in Him":

> God is with me. He is my Source of life, the life within, the air I breathe, the food by which I am sustained, the water which renews and cleanses me. He is my home, wherein I live and move; the Spirit Which directs my actions, offers me Its Thoughts, and guarantees my safety from all pain.
>
> (W-pII.222.1:1–3)

This passage provides a wonderful explanation of how God is with us; that is, as long as you understand that life, air, food, water, and home do not refer to the body, but instead are symbols referring to our true condition in Heaven. He is "the life within" means that God is the Spirit that animates my spirit, that gives life to my being. He is "the air I breathe" means, God is the spiritual "air" that my spirit breathes in Heaven. Likewise, He is the spiritual "food" which sustains me in Heaven. He is the spiritual "water" which I "drink" in Heaven and which "cleanses me" — keeps me holy. "He is my home" means not that my body lives within Him, but that my mind is quite literally a Thought inside of His Mind. These concrete symbols make this passage a great one to repeat slowly and consciously, focusing on the true meaning of each phrase. You may even want to memorize it.

All of that falls within my first answer above for how God could be with us. It says that God is my Source, home, and substance from which I can never be separate, even if I dream that I am somewhere else and someone else. The final part of the passage, however, refers to my second answer above. It says that God is "the Spirit Which directs my actions, offers me Its Thoughts, and guarantees my safety from all pain." This clearly refers to the Holy Spirit, Whom the Course says does accompany us on our journey in a very specific way. The Holy Spirit does "walk" with us. However, this passage says that "God is...the Spirit Which directs my actions." God is the Holy Spirit! To put it differently, God walks with us *through* His Holy Spirit.

The benefits of God
being with us

The idea of God being with us is expressed in many ways in the Course, as God going with us, leading us, being near us, beside us, around us. The principle image appears to be God walking with us. In its different forms, this idea is a major teaching of the Course, one that has been largely overlooked because, I think, of how traditional and dualistic it sounds. Why is this idea so important in the Course? Why is it helpful to think of God walking with us?

To answer this question we will turn to two paragraphs from Lesson 41, "God goes with me wherever I go." This (along with Lesson 156) is one the primary Workbook lessons to stress this idea.

> Today's idea will eventually overcome completely the sense of loneliness and abandonment all the separated ones experience. Depression is an inevitable consequence of separation. So are anxiety, worry, a deep sense of helplessness, misery, suffering and intense fear of loss. (W-pI.41.1:1-3)

The opening sentence of this paragraph claims remarkable benefits for this idea. Imagine one idea utterly banishing all sense of loneliness and abandonment in everyone! We immediately wonder how it can do this. How can the idea that God goes with us have such profound effects? The next lines provide the beginnings of an answer. They say that human suffering is the product of separation, separation from God. Look at all the symptoms of separation that are listed in this paragraph. When we feel separate from God, we feel lonely and abandoned, for we are apart from our Love. We are also depressed, for, cut off from our Father, everything looks bleak. We also feel anxious, worried, and helpless, because God was our strength and safety, and He is gone. In short, we feel that we have lost everything, and we fear that still more loss is on the way.

The idea that "God goes with me wherever I go" is the antidote for all this for a very simple reason: It claims that separation does not exist. The One we feel separate from is right here. He is with us now. He goes with us wherever we go. We are not separate from Him at all. In other words, "God goes with me wherever I go" is another way of saying that the separation never happened! Let's move on to Paragraph 4 of this lesson:

> You can never be deprived of your perfect holiness because its Source goes with you wherever you go. You can never suffer because the Source of all joy goes with you wherever you go. You can never be alone because the Source of all life goes with you wherever you go. Nothing can destroy your peace of mind because God goes with you wherever you go. (W-pI.41.4:1-4)

This important paragraph lists four particular benefits that come from the idea that "God goes with you wherever you go." These four are: incorruptible holiness, protection from suffering, unfailing companionship, and unassailable peace of mind. They all come because their Source goes with us. This clues us in on why God going with us holds such benefits. Think about the idea of being with someone. Why is it pleasurable to be with someone you love? When you are with a loved one, all that he has to give he can give you. This includes the things he is trying to give you, like his love, his helpfulness, his companionship. It also includes the gift of who he is, the pleasure of being around his talents and positive character traits. He doesn't *actively* give you this gift. You simply soak it in by osmosis. He "gives" it to you by his mere presence.

Now let's apply this to God. If God is with you, then everything He has to give you, He can, and He *is*. And what, according to the Course, does God want to give you? Everything. He wants to give you eternity, infinity, the Sonship, Heaven, all of His Love, all of His knowledge, all of His joy, all of *Himself*. The Course reminds you of this again and again: "His Fatherhood gave you everything" (T-10.V.13:7). "God gave you all there is" (T-29.VIII.9:7). *"God has given you everything"* (T-4.III.9:2).

If God is with you now, then this act of giving is occurring right now. At this very moment, He is giving you everything. And you can experience Him doing so, if you truly believe He is with you. Otherwise, you will believe He is too far away to give you His gifts, and this will put up a barrier in your mind that shuts them out. That is why the idea that God goes with you can deliver such unparalleled benefits. That is why, as this lesson opened by saying, it can "overcome completely the sense of loneliness and abandonment all the separated ones experience."

PRACTICING THE IDEA THAT GOD
WALKS WITH YOU

Again in Lesson 41, let's now take a look at Paragraph 10:

> Throughout the day use today's idea often, repeating it very slowly, preferably with eyes closed. Think of what you are saying; what the words mean. Concentrate on the holiness that they imply about you; on the unfailing companionship that is yours; on the complete protection that surrounds you.
>
> (W-pI.41.9:1-3)

Finally, we come to the practice of this idea. Having seen the benefits it can bring if truly internalized, how *can* we internalize it? This paragraph provides some very practical instruction. We can outline this instruction as follows:

- *Repeat the idea ["God goes with me wherever I go"] often throughout the day.*
- *Repeat it very slowly.*
- *Repeat it with eyes closed if you can.*
- *While repeating it, think about the meaning of the words.*
- *Concentrate specifically on the holiness, unfailing companionship, and complete protection (three of the four things from our earlier list) implied by this idea.*

So why not give this a try right now? Close your eyes and repeat this idea *very slowly:* "God goes with me wherever I go." Dwell on each word as you do. Then repeat it slowly again, this time thinking about how holy you must be if God is with you imparting to you His holiness. Then repeat it again, thinking about the "unfailing companionship that is yours." Then again, thinking about the "complete protection that surrounds you."

Now imagine that you were doing this several times an hour all day long. Do you think it would have an effect on your state of mind? Do you think it would have an effect on your sense of relationship with God?

Practicing this idea is everything. It does us very little good to simply read that God goes with us wherever we go. Our minds don't really believe it. It is just a theory to us. To bring it from a mere theory to a lived experience takes one thing: practice. In the rest of this chapter, therefore, I will discuss some of the ways in which the Course has us practice this idea.

"Here I am, Lord"

The first way is from outside of the Course; actually, from *before* the Course. The day before the Course itself started coming through Helen Schucman, she received guidance from Jesus about Bill Thetford. In this guidance, Jesus gave Bill a particular practice designed to help Bill feel present—present to himself and present to God. That practice is the repetition of the phrase "Here I am, Lord." This phrase does not mean, "Hey there, Lord, I'm over here (in this spot, in this world)." The "here," in other words, does not refer to a physical location. It does not denote where you are physically present, but to *Whom* you are *mentally* present. "Here I am, Lord" means, "I am present to You, Lord." Perhaps a good concrete analogy is when an employee has been summoned by a boss and he arrives saying, "Here I am, sir."

Jesus, however, suggested more than simply that Bill use this phrase. He provided specific instructions in how to practice it. Here is what he said, as recorded in *Absence from Felicity*, by Ken Wapnick (p. 197):

- [Use] a very short phrase like "Here I am Lord"
- and don't think of *anything* else.
- Just pull in your mind slowly from everywhere else
- and center it on these words.

The power of this simple practice is something one could never guess without trying it. So again I suggest that you try this one out for yourself. To really appreciate it, give yourself perhaps two or three minutes in which to practice it. Simply close your eyes and empty your mind. Pull it in from its scattered thoughts about the outer world and center it on this phrase, "Here I am, Lord." Repeat the words slowly and say them directly to God. Then repeat them again. Allow yourself time to savor each repetition; pause after each one and give it time to sink in. Then repeat the phrase again, continuing to do so until the two or three minutes are up.

Hearing Him say, "I am Here"

A related practice is recommended in Lesson 153. In its context it refers to Christ, but we can also read it as referring to God:

> We will remind ourselves that He remains beside us through the day, and never leaves our weakness unsupported by His strength. We call upon His strength each time we feel the threat of our defenses undermine our certainty of purpose. We will pause a moment, as He tells us, "I am here." (W-pI.153.19:4–6)

This passage actually refers to two different practices. The first is reminding ourselves throughout the day "that He remains beside us." We already discussed this practice in relation to Lesson 41, which instructed us to remind ourselves all day long that "God goes with me wherever I go." The second practice is what concerns us now. We can outline that practice as follows:

- Each time during the day that we feel threatened and defensive
- we call upon God's strength (which we have been reminding ourselves is right there beside us),
- pause a moment,
- and hear Him tell us, "I am here."

I am not one of those people that actually hears God say to me, "I am here." So I just *imagine* Him saying that to me, and that works well enough. I find that this practice, aside from effectively calming fear, is a great counterpoint to "Here I am, Lord." It is as if God is answering our statement of being present to Him with His statement of being present to us.

The frequency of practice

The final practice I want to look at in detail concerns the question of how often to practice this idea that God walks with us. I already alluded to this practice earlier in the chapter. This comes from Lesson 156:

> "Who walks with me?" This question should be asked a thousand times a day, till certainty has ended doubting and established peace. Today let doubting cease. (W-pI.156.8:1–3)

This suggests, in so many words, that you should ask this question, "Who walks with me?", once a minute all day long (we are awake roughly a thousand minutes a day); and that you should keep doing so until the day the answer ("God") dawns on you with certainty and puts all your doubts and anxieties forever to rest.

Additional practices

What follows are sentences the Course gives us for practicing this crucial idea. One thing I recommend is to simply go down this list, spending time with each one until it causes a shift in your mind, and then going on to the next.

Here I am, Lord.	(Absence from Felicity, p. 197)
God goes with me wherever I go.	(W-pI.41.Heading)
I walk with God in perfect holiness.	(W-pI.156.Heading)
Who walks with me?	(W-pI.156.8:1)
God is with me. I live and move in Him.	(W-pII.222.Heading)
Your peace is with me, Father. I am safe.	(W-pII.245.Heading)
I am surrounded by the Love of God.	(W-pII.264.Heading)

My heart is beating in the peace of God.　　　　(W-pII.267.Heading)

God is with me. I cannot be deceived.　　　　　　(M-16.10:5–6)

I walk with God in perfect holiness.
I light the world, I light my mind and all
the minds which God
created one with me.　　　　　　　　　　　　(W-pI.156.8:5–6)

Today the peace of God envelops me.
And I forget all things except His Love.　　　　(W-pII.346.Heading)

I have no cause for anger or for fear,
For You surround me. And in every need
That I perceive Your grace suffices me.　　　　(W-pII.348.Heading)

CONCLUSION

In this chapter I have attempted to present the concept that God walks with us as both a profound idea and a powerful practice. At first, we may be tempted to think it sounds too much like old-time religion. Yet as the Course presents it, this idea is actually a deep expression of the Course's non-dualistic foundation. This foundation says that the entire scenario in which we left God, and so must journey to reunite with Him, is an illusion. It never happened. This is an exceedingly lofty thought. Yet, oddly enough, the idea that God walks with us says the exact same thing. For if God is with us now then we never actually left Him and we are already back with Him. If God is with us right now then the problem never occurred, the journey is an illusion, and the goal is already achieved. And this is what we will experience if we practice this idea diligently and consistently, to the point where we open our minds to the full reality of it and feel God with us, beside us, surrounding us, at one with us.

Perry & Watson

11

PRAYER

Allen

Do We Pray to God, Jesus, or the Holy Spirit?

When we talk about prayer, the question naturally arises: Who are we praying to? Do we pray to God the Father, to Jesus, to the Holy Spirit, or are we perhaps (as some have suggested) actually just engaging in a kind of monologue with our own minds?

Most of the examples of prayer that we have in the Course are directed to God the Father. The prayers in Part II of the Workbook, one in every lesson, are the main evidence here. Almost every prayer begins with the word, "Father." There is only one clear example that I know of giving a prayer that is directed to the Holy Spirit: Lesson 358, which begins by addressing the Holy Spirit but then switches to the Father. The "Final Lessons," 361 to 365, also begin with a prayer that seems to address the Holy Spirit. None of the prayers in Part II address Jesus. Clearly, then, the general expectation is that our prayers should be directed to God Himself.

Prayer is communication with God. The Course views a lack of communication with God as *unnatural* (T-14.III.18:1), and says,

> It is quite possible to reach God. In fact it is very easy, because it is the most natural thing in the world. (W-pI.41.8:1–2)

Prayer, therefore, is entirely in accord with the Course's thought system; in fact, in this world, it is the most natural thing in the world. According to the Course, prayer will always have a place in our lives until we pass beyond perception to full, intimate *knowledge* of God:

> As long as perception lasts prayer has a place. Since perception rests on lack, those who perceive have not totally accepted the Atonement and given themselves over to truth. Perception is based on a separated state, so that anyone who perceives at all needs healing. Communion, not prayer, is the natural state of those who know. God and His miracle are inseparable.
>
> (T-3.V.10:1–5)

In other words, prayer does belong to "a separated state." It is communication between two apparently separate persons, ourselves and God. In the state of knowledge, there are not two, but One: "God and His miracle are inseparable." Therefore, prayer has no more place. (In *The Song of Prayer*, the definition of prayer is expanded to include the state of "communion" mentioned above, although still with a suggestion of relationship. That "song of prayer" is the highest expression of prayer, which "rises as a song of thanks to your Creator, sung without words, or thoughts, or vain desires, unneedful now of anything at all" (S-1.II.7:8).) But here and now, prayer *does* have a place. In fact, it serves the purpose of restoring us to full communion with God Himself.

There are clear indications in other parts of the Course, however, of prayers to the Holy Spirit or to Jesus. For instance:

> Ask me which miracles you should perform. (T-1.III.4:3)

First person references such as "Ask me" in the Course refer to the author, that is, Jesus. If I ask Jesus which miracles to perform, that certainly can be considered to be a prayer to Jesus. So prayers to Jesus are clearly "okay." In fact, in discussing the role of Jesus, the Course says:

> The name of Jesus Christ as such is but a symbol. But it stands for love that is not of this world. It is a symbol that is safely used as a replacement for the many names of all the gods to which you pray.   (M-23.4:1–3)

Clearly, then, praying to Jesus is acceptable practice for students of the Course. The same is true of prayers to the Holy Spirit. The following are just two of many examples of asking, or prayer, directed to the Holy Spirit:

> When the ego tempts you to sickness do not ask the Holy Spirit to heal the body, for this would merely be to accept the ego's belief that the body is the proper aim of healing. Ask, rather, that the Holy Spirit teach you the right *perception* of the body, for perception alone can be distorted.   (T-8.IX.1:5–6)

> You do not know what it [God's Will] is, but the Holy Spirit remembers it for you. Ask Him, therefore, what God's Will is for you, and He will tell you yours.   (T-11.I.8:6–7)

Ultimately, all prayer must be to God, since God, in the end, is All there is. Jesus and the Holy Spirit are simply God's Messengers or Ambassadors; They speak for God, and They listen on His behalf as well. Since the Course gives no specific directions along these lines, but has examples of prayers to all three — Father, Holy Spirit, and Jesus — in my judgment the choice is left to us. What are we most comfortable with? What serves us best? What seems most meaningful to us? If addressing our prayers to Jesus or the Holy Spirit seems most natural at times, we should feel free to do so. There is no rule, no right or wrong about it. Yet it seems to me that ultimately the goal is to get us back into communication with our Creator, with God.

Therefore, if we find that we are avoiding prayer to God directly, it may be we are using Jesus or the Holy Spirit as a way of keeping God at a distance. We may want to examine the fear of God that implies, and ask to be freed from it.

The Holy Spirit as Translator

Another way the Holy Spirit functions as a bridge between the formless God and ourselves is as "the Communication Link between God the Father and His separated Sons" (T-6.I.19:1). As such He plays a key part in prayer. In the Course's understanding of prayer, without the Holy Spirit, prayer would be impossible.

In one puzzling sentence, the Course tells us that God does not understand our words:

> God does not understand words, for they were made by separated minds to keep them in the illusion of separation.
>
> (M-21.1:7)

We may wonder, if this is so, what is the purpose of praying? If God does not understand our words, what in Heaven's name are we doing, spouting words to God? The Course explains that, though God does not understand the words, He *does* hear our prayers and answers them, because the Holy Spirit acts as interpreter:

> Never forget that the Holy Spirit does not depend on your words. He understands the requests of your heart, and answers them. Does this mean that, while attack remains attractive to you, He will respond with evil? Hardly! For God has given Him the power to translate your prayers of the heart into His language. He understands that an attack is a call for help. And He responds with help accordingly. (M-29.6:1–7)

Our words, we are told, are really only symbols that "stand for the experiences that are hoped for" (M-21.2:6). The Holy

Spirit understands what those hoped-for experiences are, and He answers, not the words, but the prayers of the heart. He interprets our prayers to God, and interprets God's Answer to us:

> God can communicate only to the Holy Spirit in your mind, because only He shares the knowledge of what you are with God. And only the Holy Spirit can answer God for you, for only He knows what God is. (T-14.IV.10:3–4)

Thus, the *Song of Prayer* booklet actually refers to prayer as an avenue of approach to God that is *offered to us by the Holy Spirit* (S-1.I.1:1). It is the Holy Spirit Who makes prayer possible.

Different people react differently to the Course's teaching about the Holy Spirit and prayer. For some, it is a welcome relief. They have felt themselves to be so very different from God, so unable to communicate with God, that the presence of a Translator is accepted as a great gift, bridging the unbridgeable gap. Others of a more philosophical leaning may have ascribed such lofty characteristics to God—perfection, formlessness, and the like—that communication between God and such ephemeral characters as ourselves seems impossible. For them, too, the Holy Spirit is a much-needed link between the world's duality and Heaven's oneness. For still others, who with simple faith have always prayed to God and felt heard by Him, the explanation of *how* that happens via the Holy Spirit seems completely extraneous—and perhaps, for them, it is.

The main point is, God hears and answers our prayers. Prayer is our communication with God, and reestablishing our communication with God is one of the stated goals of *A Course in Miracles.* One sign that we are "learning" the Course, then, would obviously be an increasingly active prayer life. More and more, our minds would be in communication with God, speaking with Him, and listening to His Voice in all things.

THE LEVELS OF PRAYER

How, then, should we pray? *The Song of Prayer* speaks of various levels of prayer, like rungs on a ladder. It talks of different types of prayer at each rung of the ladder. The fact that some rungs are below others and some are above does not make any rung more important than another, however. The lower rungs are not less important or less spiritual. First grade in school is not less important than sixth grade; in fact, since so many foundational things are taught in first grade, it could be argued that it is the most important grade. This is true in prayer as in school; without the lowest rungs you would never be able to reach the higher rungs; all of the rungs are important.

1. Asking Out of Need

This is the form of prayer we are most familiar with from traditional religions: asking for things. Simply *wanting things* is a kind of "prayer as asking." It is an unavoidable form of prayer:

> No one, then, who is sure of his Identity could pray in these forms. Yet it is also true that no one who is uncertain of his Identity can avoid praying in this way. (S-1.II.2:2–3)

In other words, don't kid yourself. If you are uncertain of your Identity — and who among us is not? — you will be praying this kind of prayer whether or not you frame it as actual prayers in words. Just wanting out of a sense of scarcity is "prayer as asking."

For myself, if I am feeling lack or scarcity, even though intellectually I know it is false, I would rather bring that sense of scarcity to God than try to handle it on my own! So sometimes I ask God for things — for more money, for a better relationship, or for new computer equipment. I know very well that things are not what I really want and need to make me happy. But emotionally, I still *want* them. Whether I put my prayers into words or not, I am praying for them. In *consciously* bringing my desires to God, the Holy Spirit will translate them into the prayer of my heart, and I'll get what I need, not what I think I want. For me, this is a form of communion with God, a way of "casting all my cares" on Him.

> Do you really believe you can plan for your safety and joy better than He can? You need be neither careful nor careless; you need merely cast your cares upon Him because He careth for you.   (T-5.VII.1:3–4)

2. Higher Asking, With Lingering Guilt

The Song of Prayer identifies the second level as a higher form of asking out of need, in which we have an unstable sense of identity with God, blurred by our deep-rooted sense of sin. At this level, we may elevate our prayers above mere wanting of things, and "ask for gifts such as honesty or goodness, and particularly for forgiveness for the many sources of guilt" (S-1.II.3:4). This is a common kind of prayer, probably familiar to many of us. We ask to be better people and to be forgiven by God for our sins. I know this level sounds very familiar to me!

We need to accept that this and the preceding level *are valid levels of prayer.* If you have little sense of Identity in God, or if you have only a beginning awareness of your oneness with God, and a lot of guilt still comes up, these are the levels of prayer you are going to be practicing. And that is fine, there is nothing to be ashamed of, any more than a six-year-old should be ashamed of doing addition and subtraction problems instead of algebra.

> Prayer in its earlier forms is an illusion, because there is no need for a ladder to reach what one has never left. Yet prayer is part of forgiveness as long as forgiveness, itself an illusion, remains unattained. Prayer is tied up with learning until the goal of learning has been reached.   (S-1.II.8:3–5)

We all need to pray. We cannot begin our prayers at the top of the ladder! Some of us still need to pray out of need, to pray through our guilt. If we try to avoid these forms of prayer, think-ing they are beneath us, we will probably end up avoiding prayer altogether! If you try not to step on the lower rungs, you proba-bly won't get up the ladder.

3. Enmity Replaced by Friendship

In *The Song of Prayer*, this is seen as "a means for lifting your projections of guilt from your brother, and enabling you to rec-ognize it is not he who is hurting you" (S-1.III.1:4). Jesus points out that at the earlier levels, one thing you asked for was very likely vengeance on your brothers! Now, you begin to let go of the idea that your brother is your enemy. It begins with these thoughts;

> What I have asked for my brother is not what I would have. Thus have
> I made of him my enemy. (S-1.III.3:5–6)

Here, you begin to see value in setting other people free of their guilt. You want for others what you want for yourself. You pray in order to forgive; you ask the Holy Spirit to help you end your projection and see your brother sinless because you want to see yourself that way.

4. Joining in Prayer

Now, you share in prayer. Praying with other people is encouraged by the Course. Not just physically getting together to pray, but really joining with another mind in a common goal. "We go together, you and I," is the thought that initiates this level (S-1.IV.1:8). Yet even as we join in prayer, we may still dip into the lower levels:

> Yet it is likely at first that what is asked for even by those who
> join in prayer is not the goal that prayer should truly seek. Even
> together you may ask for things…You may ask together for
> specifics, and not realize that you are asking for effects without
> the cause. (S-1.IV.2:4–6)

Often, such misguided prayers will appear to us to be unan-swered: "And this you cannot have" (S-1.IV.2:7). This next level of praying demands that we get past specifics, if for no other reason than that every one of us will have different specifics. Only God can give an answer in which "all separate wishes [are] unified as one" (S-1.IV.3:2).

This level of prayer requires that we learn, together, to seek the guidance of the Holy Spirit: "What is the Will of God"? (S-1.IV.3:1). Rather than praying for specific things, for our ideas of what ought to happen, we learn not to "restrict" our asking. We begin to go for the gold, so to speak; to ask for the *cause* rather than the *effects*. We pray to have the peace of God.

At this point, let's look more closely at this particular kind of asking prayer: *praying for guidance.*

Guidance

Asking for guidance is closely akin, I think, to asking in general, but it is definitely a step above, in that it does not necessarily proceed from sense of scarcity. It is more like a recognition that we cannot guide ourselves. We are instructed to ask God to guide us very specifically, in many, many ways. This is something the Course encourages us to do all through the day. For instance, we ask during our daily quiet time of spiritual practice:

> Remembering this, let us devote the remainder of the extended practice periods to asking God to reveal His plan to us. Ask Him very specifically:
>
> *What would You have me do?*
>
> *Where would You have me go?*
>
> *What would You have me say, and to whom?*
>
> (W-pI.71.9:1–5)

We are praying here for our day, asking God to guide us. More than that, we are asking Him for specific directions about what to do, where to go, and what to say to whom. Chapter 30 in the Text opens with an exercise which directs us to, *every day,* begin the day by determining to make no decisions by ourselves, but to make *every decision* with the Holy Spirit. That is a powerful lot of asking! Perhaps asking God to lead us reminds us of old-fashioned or childish religions. Well, it *is* childlike, but in a good sense:

> The Bible tells you to become as little children. Little children recognize that they do not understand what they perceive, and so they ask what it means. (T-11.VIII.2:1–2)

We don't know how to interpret anything we see; we need help. We need to ask God to guide us. The following quotes state this clearly, and they are only a small sample of many similar quotations in the Course. Learning to be guided by God's Voice is one of the primary learning goals of *A Course in Miracles*.

> It will never happen that you must make decisions for yourself. You are not bereft of help, and Help that knows the answer.
> (T-14.III.11:1–2)

> You know not of salvation, for you do not understand it. Make no decisions about what it is or where it lies, but ask the Holy Spirit everything, and leave all decisions to His gentle counsel.
> (T-14.III.12:5–6)

> Without His guidance you will think you know alone, and will decide against your peace as surely as you decided that salvation lay in you alone....Forget Him not and He will make every decision for you, for your salvation and the peace of God in you. (T-14.III.14:4,7)

This sort of asking for guidance will, like other forms of asking for specifics, eventually be left behind. Prayer evolves towards formlessness, and the farther we go, the less we will be asking for specific guidance, and the more we will be simply giving ourselves into the hands of Love, trusting that Love to take us wherever It will.

5. Beyond Separation; True Humility

The last rung of the ladder of prayer is praying only for what we truly share. Here, we say, "I cannot go without you, for you are a part of me" (S-1.V.3:9). At the top, we recognize our union with one another, and our prayer is a celebration of our shared Identity in Christ. Many of the latter prayers of the Workbook are of this kind, filled with gratitude and thanks to God.

6. Beyond Levels: The Song of Prayer

At the top of the ladder, there is no asking at all:

> For now it rises as a song of thanks to your Creator, sung without words, or thoughts, or vain desires, unneedful now of anything at all. So it extends, as it was meant to do. And for this giving God Himself gives thanks. (S-1.II.7:8–10)

These higher levels are beautiful, and I think we do need to practice them, just as the Course encourages the practice of the holy instant (T-15.II.5). Else, how will we ever make them ours? I believe many of the later lessons in the Workbook, which sometimes seem to aim far above our heads and far beyond our level of experience, are just such practice sessions, a sort of spiritual stretching practice. Yet, when it comes to levels of prayer, my advice is: Don't be pretentious. Do not pretend to a higher level of spiritual development than is really yours. Pray at the level where you feel the deepest needs exist, until you learn without a doubt those needs are illusions. While they seem real, bring your needs to God in prayer. He will hear, and He will answer.

OTHER FORMS OF PRAYER

Not all prayer is some kind of asking; prayer can take many different forms.

Prayer as Giving Thanks (Gratitude)

Often, prayer can simply be a way of expressing our gratitude towards God. The Course explains that God does not need our gratitude, but that we do need it! (see T-6.I.17:1–2) There are many examples of prayers of gratitude in the Course:

*I thank You, Father, **for the many gifts** that come to me today and every day from every Son of God. **My brothers** are unlimited in all their gifts to me. Now may I offer them my thankfulness, that gratitude to them may lead me on to my Creator and His memory.*

(W-pII.315.2:1–3, emphasis mine)

*Father, I thank You **for today, and for the freedom I am certain it will bring**. This day is holy, for today Your Son will be redeemed. His suffering is done. For he will hear Your Voice directing him to find Christ's vision through forgiveness, and be free forever from all suffering. Thanks for today, my Father. I was born into this world but to achieve this day, and what it holds in joy and freedom for Your holy Son and for the world he made, which is released along with him today.*

(W-pII.340.1:1–6, emphasis mine)

Declaring the Truth
(Asking For What We Already Have)

Another kind of prayer that occurs often in the Workbook is simply declaring the truth, which is a way of asking for what we already are and have.

True prayer must avoid the pitfall of asking to entreat. Ask, rather, to receive what is already given; to accept what is already there.   (S-1.I.1:6–7)

The many lessons that begin "Let me remember…," for instance, are this kind of prayer. Here is another example:

My true Identity is so secure, so lofty, sinless, glorious and great, wholly beneficent and free from guilt, that Heaven looks to It to give it light. It lights the world as well. It is the gift my Father gave to me; the one as well I give the world. There is no gift but this that can be either given or received. This is reality, and only this. This is illusion's end. It is the truth.

(W-pII.224.1:1–7)

This is a kind of declaration of truth. Often we are admonished to *ask for vision*, to ask for true perception, to ask to see things differently. Here, we are declaring that we know what the truth is, because God has told us.

Enjoying Relationship With God

At the higher levels, prayer becomes not so much a conversation as a loving communion, like two lovers gazing, without words, into one another's eyes:

> Prayer is a stepping aside; a letting go, a quiet time of listening and loving....And it is to Love you go in prayer. Prayer is an offering; a giving up of yourself to be at one with Love. There is nothing to ask because there is nothing left to want. That nothingness becomes the altar of God. It disappears in Him.
>
> (S-1.I.5:1,4–8)

"Giving yourself up to be at one with Love." What a beautiful way to put it. "A letting go." Just letting yourself fall back into God's embrace; just enjoying His Presence, with nothing to ask for, nothing more wanted beyond Himself.

Take a few minutes now with the prayer in Lessons 231 and 286; both of these are prayers of relationship. Let yourself feel the spirit of these prayers.

> *What can I seek for, Father, but Your Love? Perhaps I think I seek for something else; a something I have called by many names. Yet is Your Love the only thing I seek, or ever sought. For there is nothing else that I could ever really want to find. Let me remember You. What else could I desire but the truth about myself?* (W-pII.231.1:1–6)

> *Father, how still today! How quietly do all things fall in place! This is the day that has been chosen as the time in which I come to understand the lesson that there is no need that I do anything. In You is every choice already made. In You has every conflict been resolved. In You is everything I hope to find already given me. Your peace is mine. My heart is quiet, and my mind at rest. Your Love is Heaven, and Your Love is mine.* (W-pII.286.1:1–9)

If prayer is simply conversation with God, then this kind of prayer is like love-talk. "Your Love [is] the only thing I seek." "Your Love is Heaven." There is no need here but that of love to express itself.

Listening

Obviously, if we are asking God for guidance, giving our decisions to the Holy Spirit, we need to learn to listen for His answers. Not *just* for His answers, but that is definitely a part of it. Another thing we listen for is God's Word—His truth, applied personally to our own lives. The following lessons are examples of those that contain elements of listening prayer:

> We will try actually to hear God's Voice reminding you of Him and of your Self.
> (W-pI.49.3:2)

> Listen in deep silence. Be very still and open your mind.
> (W-pI.49.4:1–2)

> *Father, I come to You today to seek the peace that You alone can give. I come in silence. In the quiet of my heart, the deep recesses of my mind, I wait and listen for Your Voice. My Father, speak to me today. I come to hear Your Voice in silence and in certainty and love, sure You will hear my call and answer me.*
> (W-pII.221.1:1–5, emphasis mine)

> *Father, today I would but hear Your Voice. In deepest silence I would come to You, to hear Your Voice and to receive Your Word. I have no prayer but this: I come to You to ask You for the truth. And truth is but Your Will, which I would share with You today.*
> (W-pII.254.1:1–4)

KEEPING GOD IN OUR THOUGHTS THROUGH THE DAY

Another kind of prayer is what we might call "walking prayer." By that I mean, simply keeping God in our minds all the day long, in everything we do. The epitome of this idea is found in lesson 232:

> *Be in my mind, my Father, when I wake, and shine on me throughout the day today. **Let every minute be a time in which I dwell with You.** And let me not forget my hourly thanksgiving that You have remained with me, and always will be there to hear my call to You and answer me. As evening comes, let all my thoughts be still of You and of Your Love. And let me sleep sure of my safety, certain of Your care, and happily aware I am Your Son.* (W-pII.232.1:1–5, emphasis mine)

I recall reading, many years ago, about an 18th or 19th century Christian — it may have been George Fox, the founder of the Society of Friends — who used to greet all of his friends with the words, "Do I meet you praying?" What a concept! Imagine, expecting everyone you meet to be praying all the time, praying "without ceasing," as the Apostle Paul put it in the New Testament.

Where does prayer lead us? In the classic book *The Practice of the Presence of God*, Brother Lawrence speaks of constant, moment-by-moment practice of God's Presence. That is where prayer is leading us: back into an unceasing awareness of God.

12

Using the WORKBOOK PRAYERS

Allen

IN THE PRECEDING CHAPTER, I REFERRED TO MANY PASSAGES FROM THE PRAYERS IN PART II OF THE WORKBOOK. Robert and I feel that although most of us have cherished some of these prayers, their true significance has escaped us. At least, speaking only for ourselves, we can both say that, despite having intensively studied and taught the Course for more than a decade, it was only within the last few years that we realized the place these prayers really hold in the Workbook's training program.

Some people have felt, given the Course's emphasis on the unreality of the separation, that the presence of these prayers was somewhat of an anomaly—something peculiar and hard to explain in the light of the rest of the Course. How could God have any interest in the unreal world of illusion, or in communications from within it? I have already addressed the belief, fairly common among Course students, that there is something odd about addressing prayers to God the Father. I hope I have made it clear that the Course regards prayer as a remedial practice, a learning device that can help restore us to full, wordless communion with God. It is expected to pass away, on the one hand, and yet it is expected to remain a useful tool for us as long as perception lasts—which is to say, as long as we remain in this world!

As that understanding of the purpose of prayer began to come clear to us, one day Robert realized that the prayers of Part II in the Workbook are not just sentimental extras thrown in to make students in spiritual kindergarten feel less uncomfortable—as if Jesus were into sugar-coating the truth!—but, instead, they are key components of the training program designed "to train your mind to think along the lines the text sets forth" (W-In.1:4). Just think about it! Do you suppose, realistically, that the author of the Course would make part of each of the last 140 lessons of the Workbook consist of a practice that is meant to be discarded immediately after completing the lessons? Does that make any kind of sense? Isn't the presence of the prayers in Part II (as opposed to Part I) an indication that this is a step *up* in our training program? Something that persists right up until the end of it, just before the "Final Lessons"?

To me, it makes infinitely more sense to think that these prayers are here for a deliberate purpose, and that they are as important to us as the amount of space devoted to them would seem to indicate. They are part of the training program because it is important to teach us to pray regularly, and it is important to teach us *how* to pray. It makes sense that they are meant to be used, and that the use of them is meant as a drill to instill in us a habit of prayer that will last the rest of our life in this world.

CLUES TO THE PURPOSE
OF THE WORKBOOK PRAYERS

In the Introduction to Part II of the Workbook, there are several clear clues about how these prayers are meant to be used.

The Introduction goes into some detail about how to spend our extended morning and evening times. The focus is not on the specific words of the day's lesson as they appear in the Workbook. The words are "but...guides on which we do not now depend" (W-pII.In.1:2). The primary goal is direct experience of the truth, or the holy instant. Reading the daily lesson and repeating its main thought is only the beginning (W-pII.In.2:1); having used the words to focus our minds, we spend our time waiting for God to come to us (W-pII.In.3:3,4:6). These times are called "periods of wordless, deep experience" (W-pII.In.11:2). The bulk of our morning and evening times should be spent thus, in silent waiting and receptivity, without verbal thought.

That is what Part II of the Workbook is intended to teach us: how to enter into wordless, deep experience of God's Presence, silently waiting, open to receive whatever God wants to impart. What part do these written prayers play in that training program?

The Introduction to Part II does not specifically mention "prayers" nor how to use them, but I believe the following words actually do refer to the prayers, and give us instruction in their use and purpose:

> We say some simple words of welcome, and expect our Father
> to reveal Himself, as He has promised.   (W-pII.In.3:3)

> So our times with Him will now be spent. We say the *words of*
> *invitation that His Voice suggests,* and then we wait for Him to
> come to us.   (W-pII.In.4:5–6, my emphasis)

Finally, the Introduction itself shifts into prayer with a sort of un-self-conscious naturalness, in W-pII.In.6:2–7:8.

Those "words of invitation," suggested to us by God's Voice, are, I believe, the prayers given to us in each day's lesson. Clearly, the prayers are words, and these words are suggested for our use, to invite God to speak to us, and to offer welcome to Him. The exact words of the prayer in the lesson are not to be repeated as a ritual; they are a *suggestion* to us of how to pray. That implies that we should be free to improvise.

What are we supposed to do with these prayers? "We say some simple words of welcome." We say them. Actually speaking these prayers, praying them, can be a powerful tool in bringing us the direct experiences with God these lessons intend for us. If you want to know for yourself, just try it! When I began actually dwelling on these prayers and really *saying* them, using them as a vehicle of communication between myself and God, it had a tremendous effect on me. God's Presence became much more real to me.

What comes towards the end of the Introduction to Part II could seem to contradict what I am saying here, because it seems to discount the importance of prayer altogether, telling us "instead of prayers" to simply call on God's Name. We need to view that passage in its context, however; if we do, we will realize it is talking about the *goal* of practice, the place to which the practices suggested in Part II, which contain prayers, will lead us. It says:

> Now is the need for practice almost done. For in this final section, we will come to understand that we need only call to God, and all temptations disappear. Instead of words, we need but feel His love. Instead of prayers, we need but call His Name. Instead of judging, we need but be still and let all things be healed.
> (W-pII.In.10:1–5)

The practice periods of Part II, each introduced by a prayer, are taking us to a place where we will need no words at all to enter into God's Presence. Perhaps we will simply call His Name, and be enveloped with a sense of His Being. But we are not at that place yet. "In this final section" means, in Part II of the Workbook. And as we practice the lessons here, "we will come to understand" how to enter God's Presence without even needing any words of introduction, without any prayers. That is what we aim at learning, but we are using the prayers as learning devices to reach that place.

The morning and evening times are meant to be times of experience and not thought. Simply feeling God's Love. Simply repeating His Name in our awareness of relationship with Him. Simply being still, letting go, letting all things be healed, like a patient lying still as the Healer does His work. "Sit silently and wait upon your Father" (W-pII.In.5:5). That is the thrust of the training program in Part II. At first, we will probably find it difficult to enter into such periods of "wordless, deep experience." The prayers are designed to help us move past our resistance, to calm our fearful thoughts, and to open us to God. Eventually, through this practice, we will learn to enter God's Presence without prayers or words, simply calling on His Name.

The prayers, then, are only meant to introduce such times of silent communion with God. I am saying we need to pay more attention to them than we have been doing, and take some time to read them aloud, to chew on them a little and perhaps put the phrases into our own words, with all the feeling we can muster. I suggest that we need to use these prayers especially if our experience of doing the second part of the Workbook does not consist of day after day, morning and evening, entering into periods of wordless, deep experience with God. I don't know about you, but that has not been my experience! Since these prayers are meant to lead us into such experience, why not make use of them?

I am not recommending, however, that the morning practice periods be given over completely to prayer. The prayers, if you consider them as a group, mostly request some sort of experience of truth. For instance, consider the first two prayers in Part II, in Lessons 221 and 222. They set the tone for this section of the Workbook, and clearly they are asking for such experiences of God:

> Father, I come to You today to seek the peace that You alone can give.
> I come in silence. In the quiet of my heart, the deep recesses of my
> mind, I wait and listen for Your Voice. My Father, speak to me today.
> I come to hear Your Voice in silence and in certainty and love, sure
> You will hear my call and answer me.   (W-pII.221.1:1–5)

Father, we have no words except Your Name upon our lips and in our minds, as we come quietly into Your Presence now, and ask to rest with You in peace a while. (W-pII.222.2:1)

Clearly, the second example is doing just what the Introduction is talking about. It is using words, in a prayer, and these words are saying, "We have no words except Your Name upon our lips." It is a prayer designed to lead us beyond prayer. We need to speak the prayer, and then wait for the experience. Part II is training us to do this twice daily, and to make such a practice a lifelong habit.

I know, in my own practice, that simply sitting down and attempting to enter into a period of silent meditation for fifteen minutes or more is often difficult. The difficulty, the resistance to relaxing into God's Presence, diminishes when I begin my quiet time with a prayer. I voice my faith; I give vent to my longing; I express my love; I offer thanks to God for His promises. Whatever seems to be important. The words serve as an entry for me into that still Presence of God, and open my heart more readily to the wordless, deep experience God has waiting for me, and for all of us, every time we call on Him.

AN EXAMPLE OF PRAYER PRACTICE

Perhaps it will help to give an example of the way you can use the prayers from the Workbook. Just reading them aloud, perhaps repeating some phrases over and over if they strike you, is one obvious way they can be used and turned into your personal prayer. To be honest, I like to take even the "non-prayer" part and turn it into prayer in my own words. But I will skip that for now, and just focus on the way you can use the prayer portion and, by expanding on it and rewording it, turn it into your own prayer, customized for you. Obviously, what I can share is only *my* personal prayer. What you need to experience is *your* personal prayer. Then, you will begin to understand my enthusiasm for it!

We will use Lesson 224 as an example. I will quote the entire lesson, so you get a feel for it all, but then I will take just the second paragraph, which is the prayer, and show you how I would turn it into my own personal prayer. I may include a few concepts or phrases from the first paragraph, since the prayers usually are related closely to the rest of the lesson they occur in.

God is my Father, and He loves His Son.

My true Identity is so secure, so lofty, sinless, glorious and great, wholly beneficent and free from guilt, that Heaven looks to It to give it light. It lights the world as well. It is the gift my Father gave to me; the one as well I give the world. There is no gift but this that can be either given or received. This is reality, and only this. This is illusion's end. It is the truth.

My Name, O Father, still is known to You. I have forgotten It, and do not know where I am going, who I am, or what it is I do. Remind me, Father, now, for I am weary of the world I see. Reveal what You would have me see instead.

MY OWN PRAYER

Father, You still know my true Name, my true Identity. You haven't forgotten! Thank You! I have forgotten it, but You have not. Thank God! As long as You remember, that true Identity is always available to me; You have kept it so I can always reclaim it. I want to reclaim that true Name, my Father; I want to remember Who I am. Open my heart to remembering!

As I am, because I don't know who I am, I don't know where I am going, or what I am doing. I am really confused, Father! I am like a ship without a rudder because I have forgotten my own Name; I have forgotten Who You created me to be. Remind me today, Father, of Who I am. I really want to remember! Oh, let me be done with my resistance to You!

I am weary of the world I see. Oh, my God, how true that is! The longer I stay in it, the more weary of it I am. The struggle, the fighting, the bickering, the competition, the unfairness and pain and betrayal are too much! I am weary of the world I see. I am weary of the meaninglessness of it all. I am weary of its repetitiveness, "same old same old." I am weary of my own slowness to learn, and weary of the stubbornness of us all.

Reveal to me what You would have me see instead! Oh! What good news! There is something I can see instead of what I am seeing now! There is something different, something God wants to show me. It is my true Identity, I know. It is my true Name. Yes, Father, reveal what You want me to see! I open myself now. I come to You, silent, still, expectant. Reveal what You would have me see.

Reveal what You would have me see.

Reveal what You would have me see.

13

Three ASPECTS of our relationship with GOD

Robert

HELEN SCHUCMAN'S SUBWAY EXPERIENCE WAS ONE OF THE PIVOTAL EXPERIENCES IN HER LIFE. Though it occurred over 25 years before she began scribing the Course, it was an extremely powerful example of what the Course would later call a miracle. In this experience, Helen's perception of disgust and revulsion in a subway train gave way to an experience of a blazing light in which she "loved everyone on the train with…incredible intensity."

What has drawn my attention is the specific images she experienced in that blazing light. Here is her telling of the story, quoted from *Absence from Felicity*, by Ken Wapnick, p. 54:

> I was finding the whole situation increasingly disgusting, and closed my eyes to shut it out, feeling sick to my stomach.
>
> And then a stunning thing happened. It was very brief….An accurate account of what happened is impossible. As an approximation, however, I can say that it was as though a blinding light blazed up behind my closed eyes and filled my mind entirely. Without opening my eyes, I seemed to be watching a figure of myself as a child, walking directly into the light. The child seemed to know exactly what she was doing. It was as if the situation were completely familiar to her. For a

moment she paused and knelt down, touching the shining ground with elbows, wrists, and forehead in what looked like an Eastern gesture of deep reverence. Then she got up, walked to the right side and knelt again, this time resting her head as if leaning against a gigantic knee. The feeling of a great arm reached around her and she disappeared. The light grew even brighter, and I felt the most indescribably intense love streaming from the light to me. It was so powerful that I literally gasped and opened my eyes.

What I see in Helen's experience is a beautiful symbol of our relationship with God, presented in three different aspects. Her experience, I hope, can give us a sense, here at the close of this book, for how we ourselves can relate to God.

THE CREATOR AND THE CREATED

Helen's vision begins as she watches herself as a child walking directly into a blazing light, then kneeling down and "touching the shining ground with elbows, wrists, and forehead in what looked like an Eastern gesture of deep reverence." I love this image. It speaks to a deep need within us, a primordial need that lies at the timeless roots of our being. There is some deep urge in us to have a God, to stand in His Presence and to acknowledge Him.

Love is a self-giving. This self-giving is our only need, for it is through this that we receive. We are meant, of course, to give ourselves in love to all living things. Yet there is a way in which we can give ourselves to our Creator that we cannot to our equals. Look at this passage from the Text:

Awe should be reserved for revelation [the direct experience of union with God], to which it is perfectly and correctly applicable. It is not appropriate for miracles [in which healed perception extends from one person to another] because a state of awe is worshipful, implying that one of a lesser order stands before his Creator....Equals should not be in awe of one another because awe implies inequality.   (T-1.II.3:1-2,5)

This says that there are certain feelings that are not appropriate in relation to our equals, but that are appropriate in relation to God. It says specifically that awe and worshipfulness only make sense when there is *inequality.* Awe is when our whole self is drawn out of our open eyes as we look on that which is truly greater than us. Worship is when our whole heart goes out to that which stands qualitatively above us. In both instances, the object of our awe and worship deserves all of us *because* it is more than us. To hold anything back would imply that there was something in us greater than it.

It is not just that God is greater, it is that He created us. We can give all of ourselves to Him because He gave all of ourselves to us. To hold anything back from Him would imply that some part of us came from somewhere else. Note your reactions to the following line: "Your creations love you as you love your Father for the gift of creation" (T-8.VI.5:7). That line has such impact, I believe, because somewhere inside we innately recognize the profound and total nature of the love the created gives to its Creator. That such a love could be directed at us is therefore a breathtaking idea.

There is thus a kind of love, a kind of self-giving that only happens in relation to God, that only makes sense with God. We are to experience awe and worshipfulness only when we stand as the lesser before the greater, as the created before its Creator. And who would want to do without such feelings? Who would want to be deprived of the joy of prostrating oneself in loving adoration before one's Creator? This total giving of ourselves is true ecstasy, for ecstasy literally means to go out of oneself.

Yet for many of us this is a repugnant idea. It can feel belittling, humiliating. We are tired of the dependency and submission implied by such an image. In fact, to my reading, a great deal of today's alternative spirituality is there as an alternative to this kind of relationship to God. Many of us have sought refuge from the Western celestial hierarchy in the formless void of Eastern mysticism. The New Age movement is another such refuge, in which we try to shed these primitive notions from humanity's childhood and realize instead that we are God.

We have some pretty valid reasons for fleeing the God that we inherited from Western religion. He looked more like a stern, quick-tempered (a friend of mine would add "alcoholic") human father than a divine Being of love. Yet, I believe, there is a deeper, more fundamental reason for our desire to level the heavenly playing field. The real reason is: *This is why we left Heaven in the first place.* The Son left "because he would not accept the fact that, although he was a creator, he had been created" (T-10.V.4:3).

This is the authority problem, which the Course says is our only problem, "the only source of conflict" (T-11.In.2:3). We just couldn't handle the fact that God was God and we were His creation. We not only had to swallow Him being our Creator, we had to accept that He had created us the same as everything else. There was no way to be special, unique or even just a little bit different. What's more, we had to swallow His Kingdom—our home—as is. There was nothing we could add on, no furniture we could change or rearrange. There was no way to leave our own personal mark, our own unique signature. All we could do was extend more of the same stuff that He had already created.

Apparently, this all proved too much for us. We decided to strike out on our own. We swore never to bow our knee again. The world we see is the testimony to this rejection of divine Authority. For in this world we get to not only change things around, we get to make our "self." We get to play our own creator. And that is how we spend just about all of our time here. We shape, improve, refine, protect and maintain our personal identity. This is a deeply cherished privilege, our most sacred right. If someone else has the audacity to think that they have the right to

Perry & Watson

dictate who we are, we become "justifiably" incensed. Yet we only think they possess this power because we have projected onto them our belief that *we* have this power.

> When you have an authority problem [with an authority in this world], it is always because you believe you are the author of yourself and project your delusion onto others [thinking now that they can author you]. You then perceive the situation as one in which others are literally fighting you for your authorship. (T-3.VI.8:2–3)

As frightening as the thought is that others hold this power, our real fear comes from our belief that we hold it. This belief is quite literally the scariest thing in the world. For it is the belief that we have the power to permanently and irrevocably screw ourselves up. Imagine a mind in a greedy and near-sighted state believing it had the power to alter absolute reality, including its own fundamental nature; power, if used wrongly, to stain its soul and turn its Father's Love into hate. Just imagine the fear that this would invoke. It would be like giving a ten-year-old responsibility for the fate of the world while it hung precariously in the balance. Yet this is the condition we all think we are in. Underneath our confident exterior we are horrified with what we have done with our power. And we are terrified of what we still might do. Quite simply, we believe that we "have made a devil of God's Son" (W-pI.101.5:3).

This is where God's role as Creator is a true saving grace. This role means that, on the level of changing anything real, we are impotent. We are unable to alter our real identity in any way. We are incapable of leaving home or corrupting our innocence. We can never turn ourselves into a devil. We simply don't have that kind of power. If we did, Jesus tells us, "you would have destroyed yourself" (T-8.VI.2:5). But, thankfully, we do not. We are not God. We therefore remain exactly as God created us. This realization, says the Course, is salvation:

Its truth would mean that you have made no changes in yourself that have reality, nor changed the universe [the Kingdom]
so that what God created was replaced by fear and evil, misery
and death.   (W-pI.110.1:3)

This is cause for relief and gratitude so deep that it can only
be expressed as the figure in Helen's vision did, by bowing before
God in wordless reverence. This is what bowing to God is really
about. It is about acknowledging His gift to us of a Self so pure,
so perfect, so sublime, that we can only pour that Self out to Him
in eternal gratitude. It is about acknowledging a Power so lovingly omnipotent that It would never allow us to mar the perfect
Self It gave us. It is about admitting that though we share all
power with God, apart from Him we have absolutely no power,
no ability to change a thing. It is about gratefully conceding that
reality is, was and always will be exactly as He created it. It is
about thanking God for being our God.

THE FATHER/CHILD RELATIONSHIP

Helen's vision continues as the child got up from the ground,
"walked to the right side and knelt again, this time resting her
head as if leaning against a gigantic knee. The feeling of a great
arm reached around her...."

There is a profound love conveyed by these simple images.
How many people do you know whom you would approach and,
instead of greeting them or saying even a word, walk over to,
kneel next to and lay your head on their knee? To me the child's
action speaks of a love so assumed that it is instinctively regard-
ed as an unquestioned fact of life; a love counted on as one counts
on the ground being there; a love that one moves in as naturally
as one breathes the air. It is clear that the child is right about this
love, for in response to her gesture she feels a great arm reach
around her—I am sure without her slightest surprise.

What really strikes me is the familiarity conveyed. It is com-
municated not only by the scene we just discussed, but by the

child's whole attitude. Helen says, "The child seemed to know exactly what she was doing. It was as if the situation were completely familiar to her." In other words, this circumstance is not foreign or alien. The child is not a stranger or guest in someone else's home. Rather, she is at home. This is her natural environment, the place that was made for her, and she for it, the place she knows better than any other. This is where she belongs; where she is from and where she will always remain.

This is all the more remarkable when one remembers that the gigantic Being she is resting against is the same One she prostrated herself before just a moment ago. It is God she is acting so familiar with. It is His home that she is treating like her own. How wonderful a state of mind hers is: knowing that this is the omnipotent Creator of all that is, knowing that she owes Him her very existence, yet knowing that she is His daughter, that she belongs in His home, and that all that He has is hers, without question, without even asking.

How glorious it would be to have this state of mind. This feeling of love, this sense of being home, is the state we all long for. It is the feeling we have been looking for since time began.

> *What can I seek for, Father, but Your Love? Perhaps I think I seek for*
> *something else; a something I have called by many names. Yet is Your*
> *Love the only thing I seek, or ever sought. For there is nothing else*
> *that I could ever really want to find.*   (W-pII.231.1:1–4)

How strange it is, therefore, that something in us shies away from this love. You would think we would leap into it with all our being. Yet something in us is actually afraid to be in the presence of such all-encompassing love. The Course has a penetrating explanation for this fear: "Being unable to love, the ego would be totally inadequate in love's presence, for it could not respond at all" (T-12.IV.3:2). That is the fear, isn't it? We are afraid that all this love will be pouring at us, and we will not know what to do. We will not know how to respond. We will be impotent on our honeymoon.

Thus, underneath our shyness about receiving love is a deeper fear of our inability to give love. In a cold, loveless world this crippling deficiency seems well hidden. We maintain that we would love if we were just loved. Yet all the while we avoid being loved, for fear that it would blow our cover and reveal just how tragically inadequate we are at loving. Even those of us who feel good at giving love sense that what we give is limited and conditional, not the real McCoy.

This inability to give love is what causes our belief that we are unworthy—perhaps our most obvious reason for recoiling from love. Our reasoning here is quite natural. If we cannot give love, how can we be worthy to receive it? Being unloving causes us to feel unlovable. This belief in unworthiness takes two distinct but highly related forms.

The first form is guilt. We have observed ourselves being unloving. We have seen our attacks, our bitterness, our judgment and resentment. We then interpret this lack of love as a sin, and conclude that we must be guilty. Being guilty, we simply do not deserve to be loved; we deserve to be punished. This guilt accounts for a great deal of our conventional image of God. For our image of a guilty self naturally projects a companion image of a stern God, scowling down at us in disapproval, sending us harsh tests, demanding sacrifice and penance before we can stand in His favor.

This also leads to our internal experience of distance from God. *The Song of Prayer* talks about a stage of prayer in which a "vague and usually unstable sense of identification [with God] has generally been reached, but tends to be blurred by a deep-rooted sense of sin" (S-1.II.3:3). In other words, our sense that we are sinful directly competes with our sense of identification with God. Hence, if we did not feel sinful and unworthy of God, we would look within and immediately locate and unite with His loving Presence. If we did not feel guilty, we would instantly become an accomplished mystic.

The second form of unworthiness comes from feeling separate. By choosing separateness we have distanced ourselves from everything, God included. We observe how isolated we are, how much we look out for number one, how little sense of identity we really feel with others. As a result of this distancing of ourselves, we assume God has distanced Himself from us. Since we have become islands, we figure the mainland has retreated from us too. Just as with guilt, then, this image of a separate self produces a companion image of God. In this case it is a distant God, a cold Father, who stands aloof from us, barely noticing that we exist, as thoughtless of us "as is the weather or the time of day" (T-27.VII.8:5).

Thus, due to our own lovelessness—in the form of attack and in the form of isolation—we assume that we are not welcome in our Father's house. For we "know" that we would be greeted with either harsh retribution or cold indifference; with eons of God's pent-up anger or with the calm news that our name cannot be located on the guest list. The Course characterizes these two attitudes as the martyr and the atheist. "The atheist believes he is alone, and the martyr believes that God is crucifying Him" (T-9.I.8:4). As we saw in Chapter 1, the Course is implying that their professed beliefs are a cover for their true sentiments. The atheist boldly affirms that God does not exist, yet deep-down feels that God has abandoned him. The martyr says He loves God, but in his heart thinks that God is executing him.

Perhaps as Course students we are in a similar situation. Perhaps our professed beliefs conflict with our true sentiments. We say that God is Love, that God does not forgive because He never condemned. Yet I am sure that most of us look within and envision a God that regards us with vague disapproval or that does not regard us much at all, that is aloof and uncaring. What can we do to remedy this? There are many answers to this question, since the whole Course is aimed at healing our fear of God by undoing our guilt.

Yet one specific suggestion is to realize that our belief that God does not love us is not doing anyone any favors. It is not courtesy, since it is a rejection of God's Love, and His only need is to give His Love. It is not virtue; to reject love has never been a virtue. We are not scoring any humility points. Quite the opposite—we are arrogantly deciding that we know better than our Creator how worthy we are. And it is not natural, for we are simply stalling the inevitable. God will always love us. We can't change that. And we will always yearn for His Love. We can't change that either, for His Love is the stuff of our being. Thus, we can truly say that "God's Will and ours are really the same in this" (W-pI.70.5:1). His single need is the exact same as our single need: the need for His Love to be received by us.

Therefore, the only loving, humble and natural thing to do is exactly what the girl in Helen's vision did: walk confidently through the doors of God's temple, without asking permission, without even knocking. There we will find that all the things we feared God would see in us never even crossed His Mind. All the responses we dreaded from Him are simply not part of His Nature. He has not been waiting in anger, leather belt in hand. He has not forgotten us. He has been waiting in Love, Arms open wide in welcome, wanting only the return of His children, His treasure, wanting only to make us happy.

> In the temple, holiness waits quietly for the return of them that love it. The Presence knows they will return to purity and to grace. The graciousness of God will take them gently in, and cover all their sense of pain and loss with the immortal assurance of their Father's Love. There, fear of death will be replaced with joy of life. For God is Life, and they abide in Life.
>
> (T-14.IX.4:1–5)

JUST THE ONE

Helen's imagery reaches a briefly stated but dramatic conclusion. After the girl knelt before God and walked over and laid her head against His knee, a great arm reached around her "and she disappeared."

Perry & Watson

This disappearance is a beloved image in the Course, one that is repeated many times:

> And as he sees the gate of Heaven stand open before him, he will enter in and disappear into the Heart of God. (W-pII.14.5:5)

> Together we will disappear into the Presence beyond the veil, not to be lost but found; not to be seen but known.
> (T-19.IV(D).19:1)

> The Son of God has merely disappeared into his Father, as his Father has in him. (W-pI.169.6:5)

The significance of this image is clear. Disappearing in God means the cessation of all separate identity, all sense of me and mine, self and other. It means transcending all trace of distance between ourselves and God. It means attaining a oneness so pure and complete that "nowhere does the Father end, the Son begin as something separate from Him" (W-pI.132.12:4). Now there is no longer God and us. There is only the One.

> A sleeping mind must waken, as it sees its own perfection mirroring the Lord of Life so perfectly it fades into what it reflected there. And now it is no more a mere reflection. It becomes the thing reflected. (W-pI.167.12:3–5)

This is the experience the mystics have sought since time immemorial, calling it by many names. This is the experience the Course calls revelation: God's intensely personal revealing of Himself to us. This is the goal of the spiritual journey, the goal of life itself, the purpose of all our eons of effort and striving.

> The peace of God is my one goal; the aim of all my living here, the end I seek, my purpose and my function and my life, while I abide where I am not at home. (W-pI.rVI.205.1:3)

And yet this, too, is greeted by us with fear, a fear which takes at least two forms. First, we are afraid that this condition is going to be boring. And given that it is for eternity, it will get *really* boring. As I have remarked before, it can sound like a million years of watching snow on the TV set.

Second, and more to the point, we are afraid that losing our boundaries will mean losing our very existence. We are afraid of being annihilated in God. In this light, the prospect of our silver dewdrop slipping into the shining sea is not exactly a thrilling one. To us, it looks more like this: "the ocean terrifies the little ripple and wants to swallow it" (T-18.VIII.3:6).

According to the Course, this is our core fear, the one that keeps us stuck in our patterns, the one that gives rise to all the fears we have mentioned above. The Course maintains that you would instantly leap into God's Arms, "were you not afraid to find a loss of self in finding God" (T-29.I.9:5). Everything the ego does day-in and day-out is for one purpose: to keep itself alive, to maintain our sense of separate identity, to keep itself from dissolving in God. I suspect that our fear of being bored to death is really a cover for this deeper fear of nothingness.

Yet the Course has at least two very cogent responses to this fear. First, this condition is not the death of self. It *is* our Self. It is what we are. In response to the above line about fearing the loss of self the Course says, "Yet can your self be lost by being found?" (T-29.I.9:6) Second, the Course characterizes this condition as an expansion, not an extinguishment. By shedding the ego we merely remove the limits from our joy. A perfect illustration is in Lesson 107. There, the Course asks us to remember our happiest, most peaceful and secure moment; and then to imagine that moment becoming a permanent, even eternal, experience; and then to imagine that moment multiplied in strength 10,000 times. This, it tells us, will give us only the tiniest hint of what Heaven will be like.

To put this another way: Have you ever loved someone so much that you wanted to dissolve all separateness between you? Have you ever wanted to join with someone so intensely that you wanted to just dispense with bodies and faces and unite directly, mind to mind, heart to heart? This is what the girl in Helen's vision is doing. The love that she and her Father share is so great that it can only be satisfied by total union, by fusing into oneness, by vanishing into the same light. Her disappearance is thus the fulfillment of her love. It is not its extinction but its natural extension.

CONCLUSION

I see Helen's vision as a sublime summary of some of humanity's primary images of relationship with God. Throughout the centuries these three images have flowed through the world's spiritual traditions. We have prostrated ourselves in reverence and awe before our Creator. We have affectionately drawn close to Him as a child would rest against its loving and beloved father. And we have sought to disappear into Him as the silver dewdrop slips into the shining sea. Because Helen's vision so beautifully captures all three of these images, I have found it very helpful to use it as a focus for meditation and prayer.

Of course, these three images have often been seen as conflicting and competing. To those who want to kneel in awe, the other two images can appear blasphemous. To those who long to disappear in mystic union, the other images can seem crudely dualistic.

Yet in Helen's vision, as in the Course, there is a sense of complete harmony between all three images. I see two ways in which these images are harmonized. The first is that they represent a process of progressively drawing nearer to God. In Helen's vision, she starts with kneeling before God, then comes closer and rests against Him, then comes even closer and disappears in Him. She begins in a more distant, worshipful relationship and ends by joining with Him completely.

Yet by itself this suggests that in each stage we leave the prior, preparatory stages behind, implying that in perfect mystic union we leave behind all trace of reverent worship and loving adoration. Yet this is certainly not accurate according to the Course. This brings us to the second way to harmonize all three images: Each image *contains* the previous ones. In other words, inside that state of total oneness there still exists the loving parent/child relationship and the worshipful prostration before the Creator. The oneness contains the earlier images because it is their natural extension. It completes what they prefigured. Thus, in our union with Him we are more totally surrendered to His Power, more completely absorbed in His Love.

This idea of all three images being synthesized into one is very paradoxical and difficult to comprehend. Yet this is precisely how the Course describes Heaven. Even though Heaven is the "awareness of perfect oneness" (T-18.VI.1:6), in which "nowhere does the Father end, the Son begin as something separate from Him" (W-pI.132.12:4), it somehow still contains a *relationship* with God, Whom we adore as our Father and stand in awe of as our Creator. "What is Heaven but a song of gratitude and love and praise by everything created to the Source of its creation?" (T-26.IV.3:5). Even in the state of perfect oneness God does not stop being our God.

Can we understand this? "No; it is meaningless to anyone here" (M-14.3:9). Yet this does not mean it is not true. In fact, if we could understand it there would be a problem, for there is nothing about Heaven that we *can* understand. We can safely say, however, that if Heaven did not contain all three kinds of relationship with God, something would be missing. Heaven would not be absolute perfection. It would not be the supreme goal of life. For the need for all three is rooted too deeply within our being. It is simply part of our nature to want to give all of ourselves to our Creator, *and* to desire to live in the unconditional Love of our Father, *and* to long to unite completely with our Beloved. Of course Heaven fulfills all of these needs. That is why it is Heaven.

the **Circle** of **Atonement**

Teaching & Healing Center

· *Publications* ·

· *Products* ·

· *Services* ·

based on **A Course in Miracles**

The Circle of Atonement
Teaching and Healing Center

is a non-profit, tax-exempt corporation founded in 1993, and is located in Sedona, Arizona. It is based on *A Course in Miracles*, the three-volume modern spiritual classic, which we believe was authored by Jesus through a human scribe.

A Note from the President

Dear Student:

Our conviction at The Circle of Atonement is that *A Course in Miracles* is a gold mine of spiritual wisdom, to be mined with the greatest care and respect. As we have attempted to do this, we believe we have found an answer to the perennial question of Course students, "How do I make it practical?" Our discovery is that the Course makes itself practical; that *A Course in Miracles* is a spiritual program laid out in detail, designed to lead us step-by-step to the lofty heights of which it speaks. If we simply follow its instructions, we will become happier, more loving and forgiving people, well on our way to complete liberation.

Our materials at the Circle are meant to help the student do just that: take the Course as a program. They are designed to aid the student in the study of the Text, the practice of the Workbook, and the fulfillment of one's function as a teacher of God. We offer these materials to you in the hope that they can serve you well on your journey home.

In Peace,

Robert Perry

P.S. We are committed to making our materials available to anyone regardless of their ability to pay. Please see our financial policy.

Mission Statement

To discern the author's vision of *A Course in Miracles* and manifest that in our lives, in the lives of students, and in the world.

1 To faithfully discern the author's vision of *A Course in Miracles.*

In interpreting the Course we strive for total fidelity to its words and the meanings they express. We thereby seek to discover the Course as the author saw it.

To be an instrument in Jesus' plan to manifest his vision of the Course in the lives of students and in the world. *2*

We consider this to be Jesus' organization and therefore we attempt to follow his guidance in all we do. Our goal is to help students understand, as well as discern for themselves, the Course's thought system as he intended, and use it as he meant it to be used – as a literal program in spiritual awakening. Through doing so we hope to help ground in the world the intended way of doing the Course, here at the beginning of its history.

3 To help spark an enduring tradition based entirely on students joining together in doing the Course as the author envisioned.

We have a vision of local Course support systems composed of teachers, students, healers, and groups, all there to support one another in making full use of the Course. These support systems, as they continue and multiply, will together comprise an enduring spiritual tradition, dedicated solely to doing the Course as the author intended. Our goal is to help spark this tradition, and to assist others in doing the same.

4 To become an embodiment, a birthplace of this enduring spiritual tradition.

To help spark this tradition we must first become a model for it ourselves. This requires that we at the Circle follow the Course as our individual path; that we ourselves learn forgiveness through its program. It requires that we join with each other in a group holy relationship dedicated to the common goal of awakening through the Course. It also requires that we cultivate a local support system here in Sedona, and that we have a facility where others could join with us in learning this approach to the Course. Through all of this we hope to become a seed for an ongoing spiritual tradition based on *A Course in Miracles*.

Friends of the Circle
JOINING IN A COMMON VISION

If the vision of the Circle presented here speaks to you, we invite you to join with us in it. Ask yourself: Is this a vision I want to see promulgated in the world? Is this something I want to give my support to? If so, perhaps you would like to become a "Friend of the Circle." The benefits include:

Category 1: $60.00 per year*

- Four-issue subscription to our newsletter, *A Better Way*
- Updates and special reports every other month or so, making you an informed partner
- Support from one of our staff in your study and application of the Course
- Special materials and hand-outs on support groups, Text studies, responses to questions
- Feedback forms to give us your ideas and concerns
- Join us in our daily Workbook and meditation practice

Category 2: $130.00 per year* - Includes all of the above, plus

- Products and services, valued at a total of $70.00 (including book rate shipping fees)

*Quarterly payment plans are available for both categories,
at a slightly higher cost.*

***ALL PRICES ARE FOR U.S. ONLY, and are subject to change.
Please contact The Circle of Atonement at (520) 282-0790
for the most current information.**

TO BECOME A FRIEND OF THE CIRCLE

- Confirm the current price for the category membership you desire with the Circle.
- Write us a paragraph or two about why you want to become a Friend. What about this speaks to you?
- Take a few moments to silently join with us in purpose.
- Enclose your initial payment/donation (If you are unable to afford the amount listed, see our Financial Policy page 175).

Services Currently Offered

NEWSLETTER, BOOKS AND BOOKLETS - *A BETTER WAY* is the Circle's newsletter, published quarterly. It is primarily a teaching journal, containing articles by Robert, Allen and others, on the Course.

Our other publications, ranging in size from booklets to full-size books, are available in bookstores or directly from The Circle of Atonement. They are expositions of a theme or section from the Course.

THE LEARNING CIRCLE - This is our school for students of the Course, and is a division of the Teaching Wing. It is designed to aid students in their reading, study and understanding of the Course. The school, started in 1994, consists of introductory classes, Text study classes, and topical classes. Classes are available by correspondence following the in-person presentation of the class. Additional information is available by requesting our introductory packet (See Ordering Information, page 186.)

WORKSHOPS, SEMINARS AND RETREATS - The Circle currently offers workshops, seminars and retreats in Sedona. These are open to all individuals interested in *A Course in Miracles*. Dates and specifics are announced in every newsletter mailing (or call the Circle for more information and dates of events). Robert and Allen are available to speak at other locations by invitation.

SUPPORT SYSTEM - The Circle is currently developing a multi-faceted support system in Sedona, under the direction of Jeanne Cashin and Robert Perry. Currently in place are Support Meetings, designed to encourage sharing of how we apply Course principles to our lives, as well as Meditation Meetings, designed to facilitate the practice of the Lessons; one-on-one support for local students, as well as telephone support for students outside the local area. See Issue #18 of *A Better Way* for more information.

FINANCIAL POLICY

Our financial policy is based on a line in *Psychotherapy*, a supplement to *A Course in Miracles*: "One rule should always be observed: No one should be turned away because he cannot pay." Therefore, if you would like any of our materials or services and cannot afford them, simply let us know, and give what you are able.

The Circle is supported entirely by your purchases and gifts. Therefore, we ask you to look within to see if you might be led to support the Circle's vision financially with a donation above the list price of materials. We encourage you to give, not in payment for goods received, but in support of our present and future outreach. Please note that only amounts given over the list price are considered tax-deductible.

Please see *A Better Way*, Issue #18 for a more detailed explanation.

Our Teachers

Robert Perry began teaching in 1986 at Miracle Distribution Center in California. He has written the popular *An Introduction to 'A Course in Miracles,' The Elder Brother: Jesus in 'A Course in Miracles,'* as well as many other books and booklets on the Course. Robert is the President of The Circle of Atonement, teacher and staff writer, and has lectured extensively in the United States and abroad.

Allen Watson is a writer and teacher for The Circle of Atonement. He has written a number of books and booklets on the Course, including *A Healed Mind Does Not Plan, Seeing the Bible Differently,* the *Workbook Companion* series on the Internet and in book form, as well as co-author of *Let Me Remember You.* Before joining the Circle he published *Miracle Thoughts* newsletter and led Course study groups in New Jersey.

Books & Booklets

BASED ON *A COURSE IN MIRACLES*

An Introduction to *A Course in Miracles* – Perry; *A brief overview of the Course;* 44 pp.; **$2.00***

ACIM Interpretive Forum
"Prosperity and *A Course in Miracles"*
With Position Papers by Allen Watson and Tony Ponticello, and Response Papers by several participants, this

journal seeks to explore the Course's position on material abundance and divine supply; 47 pp.; **$5.00***

The Elder Brother: Jesus in *A Course in Miracles* – Perry; *Jesus – the most celebrated man in history. We have prayed to him, loved him, feared him. But have we really known him?*

Perry examines the historical Jesus and compares him with the author of the Course. Was the Course authored by Jesus? Perry offers his own opinion as he lets the reader come to his or her own conclusion. Fascinating and inspiring reading for anyone interested in Jesus or the Course; 184 pp.; **$8.75***

#1 Seeing the Face of Christ in All Our Brothers – Perry;
How we can see the Presence of God in others. This booklet seeks to present the Course's lofty vision of our Divine nature; 47 pp.; **$5.00***

#3 Shrouded Vaults of the Mind – Perry;

Draws a map of the mind based on ACIM, and takes you on a tour through its many levels; 44 pp.; **$5.00***

#4 Guidance: Living the Inspired Life
Perry; *Drawn from ACIM and Perry's own experience, this booklet sketches an overall perspective on guidance and its place on the spiritual path;* 44 pp.; **$5.00***

#6 Reality & Illusion: An Overview of Course Metaphysics Part I** – Perry; *Examines the Course's vision of reality, attempting to answer the question: "What is real?";* 44 pp.; **$5.00***

#7 Reality & Illusion: An Overview of Course Metaphysics Part II –** Perry; *Examines questions such as: "Why are we here?" "How did we get here?" Discusses the origins of our apparent separation from God, and how to surmount the barriers to ultimate happiness;* 52 pp.; **$5.00***

#8 A Healed Mind Does Not Plan
Watson; *Examines our approach to planning and decision-making, showing how it is possible to leave the direction of our lives up to the Holy Spirit;* 40 pp.; **$5.00***

#9 Through Fear to Love – Watson; *Explores*

two sections from ACIM that deal with our fear of redemption and with the perception of the world that results from our fearful self-perception. It leads the reader to see how we can look on ourselves with love; 44 pp.; **$5.00***

#10 The Journey Home

Watson; *Sets forth a sequential description of the spiritual journey as seen in the Course. This booklet presents a map of sorts to give us an idea of our spiritual destination and what we must go through to get there;* 64 pp.; **$5.00***

#11 Everything You Always Wanted to Know About JUDGMENT But Were Too Busy Doing It to Notice

Perry & Watson; *A survey of various teachings about judgment in ACIM: What is judgment, giving up judgment, right use of judgment, judgment of the Holy Spirit, the Last Judgment;* 59 pp.; **$5.00***

#12 The Certainty of Salvation – Perry & Watson; *An antidote to feelings of discouragement, impatience, despair and doubt that may arise for those trying to reach the* spiritual goal of the curriculum of the Course. Gathers together many of the Course's most encouraging and uplifting thoughts, reassuring us that attaining the goal is inevitable; 51 pp.; **$5.00***

#13 What Is Death?

Watson; *Our belief in death is at the core of our painful experiences in this world. The author presents philosophical* insights from the Course about the nature of death, and seeks to explain how to apply these principles in practical situations such as the death of a loved one, or facing death ourselves; 42 pp.; **$5.00***

#14 The Workbook as a Spiritual Practice – Perry; *The Workbook of* A Course in Miracles *trains us in a profound new method of spiritual* practice, and only through this practice will we realize the wonderful promises contained in the Course. This booklet is designed to help students get the most out of the Workbook, to help them find happiness through the training of their minds; 57 pp.; **$5.00***

#15 I Need Do Nothing: Finding the Quiet Center

Watson; *This phrase captures the heart of the Course's philosophy, yet it has also been the* source of endless misunderstanding. This paragraph-by-paragraph commentary on the section, "I Need Do Nothing," seeks to draw out that heart as well as clear up the misunderstandings; 57 pp.; **$5.00***

#16 A Course Glossary

Perry; *The Course employs a unique use of language in which it fills familiar terms with new meaning. This makes its* language initially confusing, yet eventually transformative. This glossary attempts to clear up the confusion. Along with Course meanings, definitions include root, conventional, and Christian meanings. Intended for both new and experienced students, both individual and group study; 96 pp.; perfect-bound; **$7.00***

#17 Seeing the Bible Differently: How *A Course in Miracles* Views the Bible

Watson; *Addresses the question, "How does the Course relate to the* Bible?" Based on the Course's own attitude toward the Bible, it recognizes both similarities and differences, and emphasizes the continuity of God's message in the two books, seeing the Course as a clearer presentation of truth, which supersedes the Bible while standing clearly in its lineage; 80 pp.; perfect-bound; **$6.00***

#18 Relationships as a Spiritual Journey: From Specialness to Holiness – Perry; *Describes the unique teaching of the Course on the subject of human relationships, that the quest for God is best accomplished in them. This requires, however, that our relationships go through profound transformation, from special relationships, based on the pursuit of individual specialness, to holy relationships, based on a truly common goal;* 192 pp.; perfect-bound; **$10.00***

A WORKBOOK COMPANION
Commentaries on the Workbook for Students
from *A Course in Miracles*
by Allen Watson and Robert Perry

A three-volume set designed to aid students of the Course in their practice and understanding of the Workbook's daily lessons. Each volume includes a commentary and a practice summary of each lesson, as well as periodic overviews of the training goals of various lessons. These are not a replacement of the lessons themselves, but are rather a companion, with explanations, personal anecdotes, and advice on how to carry out the lessons. Each volume is perfect-bound.

#19	Volume I – covers Lessons 1 - 120	(320 pp.)	**$16.00***
#20	Volume II – covers Lessons 121 - 243	(304 pp.)	**$16.00***
#21	Volume III – covers Lessons 244 - 365	(352 pp.)	**$18.00***

Special Offer

ALL THREE VOLUMES - $45.00
(Reg. $50.00)

#22 The Answer is a Miracle

Perry and Watson; A Course in Miracles *promises to teach its students miracles, and who would not want to learn that? Yet the Course redefines miracles, causing many students to simply be confused about them. This book attempts to clear up that confusion and place miracles back where they belong, at the center of the Course, where we can learn them;* 112 pp.; perfect bound; **$7.00***

#23 Let Me Remember You: God in *A Course in Miracles*

Perry and Watson; *God is a central topic in human life and in* A Course in Miracles. *Little attention, however, has been given to God by most students and teachers of the Course. This book is an attempt to remedy that situation. It is designed to help readers gain, or perhaps, regain, a sense of God's relevance and immediacy;* 192 pp.; perfect bound; **$10.00***

Source Material

FOR OUR PUBLICATIONS

The following four books are works that we encourage every student of the Course to own. By definition, a Course student owns the Course itself. But we also believe that the other three books below are highly valuable to one's journey with the Course. All of them contain additional material dictated by Jesus through Helen Schucman. For this reason, our writings draw on them frequently.

A Course in Miracles (Hardcover) **$29.95***

The Gifts of God

This volume primarily contains Helen Schucman's poetry, which Helen felt she "received" from a deeper place in her own mind, not from

the author of the Course. However, the volume closes with a fourteen-page piece, also called "The Gifts of God," which is not one of Helen's poems. Rather, it was perhaps Helen's final authentic scribing from Jesus. We, therefore, consider it part of the Course's "canon" and for that reason our publications sometimes quote from it. **$19.95***

> ***ALL PRICES ARE FOR U.S. ONLY, and are subject to change. Please contact the Circle directly for the most current information.**

Supplements to ACIM: Psychotherapy and Song of Prayer

These are two supplements to the Course, now together in one volume. They were dictated by the author of the Course to Helen Schucman after the Course's completion. The Circle's publications refer to both supplements often, as they are the same teaching as the Course from the same author. **$9.95***

Absence from Felicity, by

Kenneth Wapnick. *This excellent "Story of Helen Schucman and Her Scribing of* A Course in Miracles" *has immense historical value for its telling of the story of the Course's birth. The reason that the Circle's writings often quote from it is that it also contains a great deal of personal guidance given by Jesus to Helen Schucman and Bill Thetford. It thus provides a window onto how Jesus envisioned the Course being applied in the everyday lives of two people.* **$16.00***

The Vision
of the Learning Circle

The Learning Circle is our school for students of *A Course in Miracles*. Our vision is to aid students in their personal study of the Course. Since the Course is a book, the foundational activity for any student is simply reading the book. This is doubly so for this particular course, for it makes the study and understanding of its thought system the foundation for walking its path. As the opening line of the Workbook says, "A theoretical foundation such as the text provides is necessary as a framework to make the exercises in this workbook meaningful."

Based on the above, that one reads the book, how one reads the book, and how much one understands its thought system are all crucial. All of these provide a foundation for giving meaning to the application of the Course. The purpose of The Learning Circle is to aid and support students in all of the above things:

~ *in reading the book*

~ *in reading it in a way that mines its treasures*

~ *in understanding what it says*

~ *in seeing how this understanding applies in our lives*

Our experience has been that this reading, study and understanding are indeed the foundation for the entire path of the Course. As students become more firmly grounded in this, their experience of the Course and their ability to apply it increase exponentially.

The Correspondence School

If you are unable to attend the classes offered in person, and wish to participate in The Learning Circle program, the tape sets from the classes are available as correspondence classes. Each correspondence class consists of a reading list, a study guide, student feedback forms, and student-teacher interaction via phone, e-mail, tape recording and/or writing. At the completion of a correspondence class, the student receives a certificate of completion from The Learning Circle.

Two of our correspondence class tape sets, 101 and 102, serve as prerequisites for continuing study with The Learning Circle, either through correspondence classes or in-person seminars. For more information, please request our information packet, which outlines the school program and class offerings (see Ordering Information, page 186).

The Learning Circle

TAPE SETS

The unedited live classes given in Sedona for students participating in our school are available on audio tape. If you are simply interested in listening to the classes, but not participating in the school, you may order the tape sets (and study guides, if desired), which are described below. If you would like to participate in the Correspondence School, receiving feedback from the teachers, please request first The Learning Circle brochure on the Ordering Form, page 186.

STUDY GUIDES $ 10.00*

Study guides are available for use with all tape sets except 101. Each study guide can be used alone or in connection with its corresponding tape set. All study guides are $10.00* each. When ordering, please be sure to specify the tape set number for which you want a study guide.

101 Basic Introduction to
A Course in Miracles – Watson
Six 60-min. tapes $ 30.00*
For familiarizing students with the perspective of the Circle's instructors; offers an overview of the Course's message and thought system; the Course as a spiritual path; and more.

102 Bringing the Course to Life: Turning Study Into Experience
Perry and Watson
Eight 90-min. tapes $ 40.00*
An intensive focusing on methods and techniques for studying the Course, taking into consideration its unique presentation of its thought system.

TEXT STUDY SERIES

A detailed paragraph-by-paragraph study of the chapters specified.

201 Text Study, Chapters 1 - 3
Watson
Ten 90-minute tapes $ 60.00*
1: The Meaning of Miracles
2: The Separation and the Atonement
3: The Innocent Perception

202 Text Study, Chapters 4 - 6
Perry & Watson
Ten 90-minute tapes $ 60.00*
4: The Illusions of the Ego
5: Healing and Wholeness
6: The Lessons of Love

203 Text Study, Chapters 7 - 8
Perry & Watson
Ten 90-minute tapes $ 60.00*
7: The Gifts of the Kingdom
8: The Journey Back

204 Text Study, Chapters 9 - 11
Perry & Watson
Ten 90-minute tapes $ 60.00*
9: The Acceptance of the Atonement
10: The Idols of Sickness
11: God or the Ego

Subscriptions for *A Better Way* Newsletter

A Better Way is designed as a teaching journal for students of the Course. The suggested subscription price is $10.00* for four quarterly issues. For more information see Ordering Information on page 186.

The Learning Circle

A Better Way

Back issues of *A Better Way*
newsletter are available for
$2.00 per copy.

A list of *Reprinted Articles* by Allen
Watson and Robert Perry from other
Course-based publications is available upon request. Please mark your
interest on the Ordering Information, page 186.

Ordering Information ────────────

All publications and products listed previously are available as of this printing. ALL PRICES ARE FOR U.S. ONLY, and are subject to change. In addition, new titles become available regularly; therefore, please contact the Circle directly for the most current information.

Information is available by writing or calling us at:

The Circle of Atonement
Teaching and Healing Center

P.O. Box 4238 • W. Sedona, AZ 86340
Phone: (520) 282-0790 • Fax: (520) 282-0523
In the U.S. toll-free: (888) 357-7520 (for orders only)
e-mail: circleofa@sedona.net
Or
You can learn more and order materials directly from our website at
http://nen.sedona.net/circleofa/
Or
You can send the form below to the above address
with your information:

- -

NAME _____

ADDRESS _____

CITY_____ PROVINCE/STATE _____

COUNTRY _____ POSTAL/ZIP CODE _____

PHONE _____

❏ Please send me a packet including information on current products, newsletter subscriptions, The Learning Circle Program, and Friends of the Circle membership

❏ Please send me a free list of reprinted articles

LMR-23